Co-production and Criminal Justice

This book explores practical examples of co-production in criminal justice research and practice. Through a series of seven case studies, the authors examine what people *do* when they co-produce knowledge in criminal justice contexts: in prisons and youth detention centres; with criminalised women; from practitioners' perspectives; and with First Nations communities.

Co-production holds a promise: that people whose lives are entangled in the criminal justice system can be valued as participants and partners, helping to shape how the system works. But how realistic is it to imagine criminal justice "service users" participating, partnering, and sharing genuine decision-making power with those explicitly holding power over them?

Taking a sophisticated yet accessible theoretical approach, the authors consider issues of power, hierarchy, and different ways of knowing to understand the perils and possibilities of co-production under the shadow of "justice". In exploring these complexities, this book brings cautious optimism to co-production partners and project leaders. The book provides a foundational text for scholars and practitioners seeking to apply co-production principles in their research and practice. With stories from Australia, the United Kingdom, and Ireland, the text will appeal to the international community. For students of criminology and social work, the book's critical insights will enhance their work in the field.

Dr Diana Johns is a senior lecturer in criminology in the School of Social and Political Sciences at the University of Melbourne, where she researches and teaches across the domains of prisons and punishment, children/young people and the criminal legal system, and criminal justice knowledge production. Her book *Being and Becoming an Ex-Prisoner* was published by Routledge in 2018.

Dr Catherine Flynn is an associate professor in social work in the Faculty of Nursing, Medicine and Health Sciences at Monash University. Her area of expertise is criminal justice and social work, with a particular focus on the implications for children and families of justice policies and interventions.

Dr Maggie Hall is a lecturer in the School of Social Sciences at Western Sydney University. She is a criminologist and former criminal lawyer and social worker. Her work foregrounds the experience of the subjects of criminal justice. Her monograph *The Lived Sentence* (2017) is part of the *Prisons* series published by Palgrave MacMillan.

Dr Claire Spivakovsky is a senior lecturer in criminology in the School of Social and Political Sciences at the University of Melbourne. Her work focuses on the violent, restrictive, and coercive practices that are used to segregate and control people with disability in the community.

Dr Shelley Turner is the chief social worker at Forensicare (Victorian Institute of Forensic Mental Health). She holds adjunct academic appointments in social work at Monash University and RMIT University, and at the Swinburne Centre for Forensic Behavioural Science. Her research focuses on youth justice, adult corrections, forensic mental health, and problem-solving courts.

Criminology in Focus

Series Editor: Sandra Walklate

This series offers a space for a 'short format' book series which showcases and puts the spotlight on new research in criminology. We are interested in books that fit the 'short-form' model; for example: theoretical think pieces, developments in criminal justice policy, paradigm shifting innovations in the fields, a compelling case study that would be of interest to an international readership. We would like to attract 'big names' as well as up-and-coming scholars; all books should speak and contribute to international criminological debates and conversations.

Co-production and Criminal Justice

**Diana Johns, Catherine Flynn,
Maggie Hall, Claire Spivakovsky
and Shelley Turner**

Routledge
Taylor & Francis Group
LONDON AND NEW YORK

First published 2023
by Routledge
4 Park Square, Milton Park, Abingdon, Oxon OX14 4RN

and by Routledge
605 Third Avenue, New York, NY 10158

Routledge is an imprint of the Taylor & Francis Group, an informa business

British Library Cataloguing-in-Publication Data
A catalogue record for this book is available from the British Library

Library of Congress Cataloging-in-Publication Data
A catalog record has been requested for this book

ISBN: 978-0-367-34902-8 (hbk)
ISBN: 978-1-032-30606-3 (pbk)
ISBN: 978-0-429-32865-7 (ebk)

DOI: 10.4324/9780429328657

Typeset in Times New Roman
by Deanta Global Publishing Services, Chennai, India

Dedication
This book is dedicated to working–making–doing together, and to different ways of knowing and being in the world.
For April and Lucy.

Contents

Preface

This book was born of a graduate-level Criminology subject about research as a knowledge-producing endeavour. That subject poses questions such as: Who does research about criminal justice? Why? For whom? What is produced? Who governs the production of knowledge about crime and criminal justice? Who defines knowledge as "evidence"? How is "evidence" valued, and valorised, and what are the implications for other forms of knowledge – other versions, other experiences, other perspectives? How can/does knowledge production function as both a colonising and potentially decolonising phenomenon, force, technique or strategy?

These questions provided a starting point for this book. They also revealed a surprising lack of scholarly or practice literature on the co-production of *criminal justice* knowledge – in research, policymaking, service delivery, and practice – in Australia at least, compared to, say, the United Kingdom. Then, in early 2018, the publication of an article (co-authored by one of us), "Building Knowledge of Consumer Participation in Criminal Justice in Australia: A Case Study" by De'Ath, Flynn, and Field-Pimm, stimulated a flurry of exchanges between us – academics and practitioners working (at the time) in criminology and social work at three Australian universities – on Twitter. Where is the Australian literature on "service user" participation, we asked each other? Why are "client" voices and lived experience not counted as policy "evidence"? And how and why is Australia so far behind on this issue?

This book is the result of that subject, that article, that conversation.

Nothing about us, without us

This book is co-produced – albeit in a limited way – by us, a group of academics and practitioners, conscious of our positions of power in the production and reproduction of criminal justice "knowledge", "evidence", and "expertise". We debated whether we – as academics and practitioners – should write this book alone. We asked, is it hypocritical to produce knowledge about the co-production of criminal justice knowledge *without* anyone who has lived experience of involvement with the criminal justice system? Shouldn't we have *co*-produced this book with them?

Maybe.

While we remain uncertain in our conclusions, we felt it important to more closely examine what it means to *co*-produce criminal justice knowledge from an academic and practitioner point of view; to critically reflect on our own standpoint, as *only one of many* knowledge-holding perspectives.

As non-Indigenous settler-occupier women living and working on unceded Aboriginal land, we acknowledge our own White Eurocentric perspectives and complicity in producing and reproducing knowledge about crime, criminal justice, and criminalised people. This book is not – and is not intended to be – any sort of definitive guide for how to co-produce knowledge in and about criminal justice settings. The focus is not on "service users" or their experiences of criminal justice. Rather, this book is an exploration of co-production as a concept, a process, and a practice.

We make no claims as co-production experts in this book. Instead, we invite you to enter into critical dialogue, to ponder and consider *with* us what it means to co-produce knowledge in and about criminal justice. What or who makes the "co" in co-production? What or who makes co-producing criminal justice knowledge unique or distinct from co-production in other contexts? These are the overarching questions that we explore in this book, and particularly through the case studies. Through these examples and questions, we invite you into a state of openness, of listening and hearing, of humility and reflexivity.

Before we proceed, we need to make our own positions clear. As a group of women academics and practitioners, we bring two main disciplinary lenses into play: criminology and social work. Of course, many other disciplines contribute to the theory and practice of criminal justice (law, psychology, medicine, politics, to name a few), and each of us brings a combination of experiences and perspectives to our thinking and writing. But criminology and social work are the specific lenses we bring to this book. These disciplines (while both are broad churches) generally have different ways of thinking about and approaching criminal justice; social work typically brings a more practical focus. Criminology and social work tend to work – in Australia at least – in parallel isolation, notwithstanding strong resonance and overlap between them. Both are characterised, for instance, by a divergence between "mainstream" and "critical" approaches.

Critical criminologists and critical social workers consider the historical, political, cultural, economic, and sociological context of crime and criminalisation. Crime and crime control, and the subjectivities they bring forth, are viewed as manifestations of power relations around which societies are structured. This critical tradition firmly orients our approach in this book. For us, this means looking below the surface of things, trying to understand what is hidden, revealing underlying assumptions, and challenging accepted orthodoxies. This approach contrasts with a purely "administrative" lens, through which criminal justice is seen in instrumental terms, as a natural response to objectively given crime problems.

As a discipline, criminology has been slow to see beyond its crime-as-a-given lens and has been criticised for being politically anodyne, serving criminal justice systems and their operation, and being inherently colonial: "an imperialist science for the control of others" (Agozino, 2004: 344). The same charge has been levelled – perhaps even more powerfully – at social work (Rodger, 1988; Briskman, 2013). However, Healy (2001) highlights an important distinction between the *theory* and *practice* of critical social work, noting the oft-unacknowledged challenges social workers face in *implementing* critical agendas. Similarly, Egan (2009: 207) notes that "workers who are anti-oppressive in their practice will experience acute tensions related to their role ... associated with providing individual services to clients who may be voluntary or involuntary, while simultaneously attempting to act as agents of social change".

These are complexities faced by many academics and practitioners working within/alongside criminal legal systems. We note that, individually, we may take different positions along the abolitionist/reformist spectrum or the radical/pragmatic continuum. Nevertheless, bringing the two "rendezvous" disciplines (Young, 2003) of criminology and social work together provides a critical intellectual and practical approach to thinking about these and other challenges of co-production in criminal justice contexts.

References

Agozino, B (2004) Imperialism, crime and criminology: Towards the decolonisation of criminology, *Crime, Law & Social Change*, 41: 343–358.

Briskman, L (2013) Courageous ethnographers or agents of the state: Challenges for social work, *Critical and Radical Social Work*, 1(1): 51–66.

Egan, R (2009) Taking action: Intervention. In J. Maidment & R. Egan (Eds.), *Practice skills in social work and welfare: More than just common sense*. Crows Nest: Allen & Unwin, pp. 205–219.

Healy, K (2001) Reinventing critical social work: Challenges from practice, context and postmodernism, *Critical Social Work*, 2(1): 1–13.

Rodger, JJ (1988) Social work as social control re-examined: Beyond the dispersal of discipline thesis, *Sociology*, 22(4): 563–581.

Young, J (2003) In praise of dangerous thoughts, *Punishment & Society*, 5(1): 97–107.

Acknowledgements

We live and work on unceded land in Australia. We acknowledge the Bunurong/Boon Wurrung and the Wurundjeri people of the Kulin Nation (in Victoria), and the Darkinjung (in New South Wales), as the Traditional Owners and custodians of these lands. We pay respect to Elders, past and present, and to the deep practical wisdom of the ancestors who have held this Country for thousands of generations. They will continue to hold us all, gently, if we listen and learn.

This book is a co-production: we have worked together over months – years – to make it. As the lead author (and lover of the dash), I want to thank this amazing team for their trust, generosity, honesty, and thoughtfulness – shared over long tables and computer screens – and for listening, laughing, and learning together. Thank you, Steph Fisher, for your early work supporting this project. Thank you, too, to our families and colleagues for giving us time, and space, to co-produce this work.

Big thanks to Penny and Murray for granting us the luxury of gathering around their long table for many days of talking, thinking, eating, walking, and writing together (in between COVID-19 lockdowns). Providing us with a beautiful space by the Yarra River to work was incredibly generous and – in Catherine's words – allowed a sense of togetherness that is necessary for a book with five authors.

Catherine's reflections on the writing of this book are perceptive: how the co-writing process encapsulates our engagement with *time* – the slow time was not of our making, but maybe the extra time made for a more thoughtful product, by allowing the relational work to occur; *space* – particularly the use of the space and sitting around the table together, with Maggie on zoom on a laptop; and *identity* – it feels like the outcome of co-writing is that everyone shifts a little.

Catherine: I feel like working with you all has sharpened my thinking and helped me to reconnect a bit more with my voice in writing – perhaps becoming a little less institutionalised! Shelley: I have loved the interaction that writing this book with you (as I transferred from academia back to statutory social work practice) has given me in a real and meaningful way with the theory and practice of co-production. Maggie, grateful for the opportunity to work in a multidisciplinary way with such talented and generous women, says: We co-produced the book and the conversations we had were a living example of working together with patience and grace. Claire is grateful for the thoughtful discussions about whose voice is heard or silenced in any work we do separately or together, and for the ways that these discussions led to a book that is far more than just the sum of five different authors thinking and writing together. For me, Diana, the pooling, stretching, and expanding of our individual perspectives and styles into something bigger than its parts was the fun, the challenge, and the alchemy of co-production.

We express deep gratitude to the people we interviewed and conversed with for the case studies: Mark, Dan, Garry, the men of HMP Pentonville Prison Council, Johanna, Sinead, Fiona, Claire, Tim, Andrea, and Glenn. Your thoughtful insights and reflections provided rich material for us to deepen our own understanding of the complexities of working to co-produce knowledge in and about criminal justice; in Australia, England, and Ireland, specifically, but with lessons for other places too.

Respect and acknowledgement to the friends and colleagues with lived experience of criminal justice entanglement, with whom we have learnt so much through working–making–doing together, in other ways, outside this book. And finally, thanks to the Twitter community for so many ideas and opinions on co-production and criminal justice. All these conversations – real and virtual – have informed our thinking and discussions throughout the writing of this book.

Part 1

1 Co-production and criminal justice

co- [*prefix*]
1. together; joint or jointly; mutual or mutually
2. indicating partnership or equality

Co-production – at its simplest "an approach to working together in equal partnership and for equal benefit"[1] – is well established in various social service settings. In health, mental health, disability, youth services, alcohol and other drug treatment settings, for instance, service users have played some role in programme design or delivery, research or evaluation for decades. These services sometimes overlap with criminal justice. But co-production in and about criminal justice *specifically*, in Australia at least, is really only just starting to gather momentum. Indeed "users" of criminal justice "services" are not so easily identifiable; are we talking about victims, "offenders", the community to be kept safe? And precisely what co-production *is*, and what it is not, isn't always clear. Arguably, many practices and principles included under the co-production umbrella have long been accepted as standard in social work as well as in community development, participatory and emancipatory research, and feminist and Indigenous approaches to knowledge. So, what exactly is co-production and what are the implications of its emergence in criminal justice?

This book is about the co-production[2] of criminal justice knowledge,[3] specifically in Australia, but with lessons from and for other places. Under the broad heading of co-production, we observe a diverse range of practices and approaches. We seek to illustrate some of this diversity and to distinguish co-production as having particular tensions and characteristics when it is undertaken in criminal justice contexts. We recognise that many people use criminal justice services, but we focus predominantly in this book on people who have been criminalised. We locate our analysis mainly in the Australian context, because we live and work here, but also because we observe co-production practice burgeoning in a range of criminal

DOI: 10.4324/9780429328657-2

justice-related settings, yet with a notable scarcity of accompanying scholarly discussion.

As a settler colony, Australia offers a unique perspective on the politics and possibilities of co-producing knowledge with, for, and about people involved in the criminal justice system. The most conspicuous example of this is the way Australia's settler-colonial history and the impact of colonisation continues to shape the experience of Aboriginal and Torres Strait Islander peoples[4] today. The disproportionately high rates of Indigenous peoples' incarceration in Australia exceeds that of First Nations peoples in Canada, Māori in New Zealand, and of both Native and African Americans in the United States (Anthony & Baldry, 2017). Against this background, we consider the imperatives of criminal justice reform and the role of knowledge production (and producers) in maintaining the status quo and/or moving towards genuine structural change. *Co*-production holds the promise and possibility of working together, in partnership, with shared power; and not only valuing the voices and perspectives of those with lived experience of justice-system involvement but supporting their active participation and leadership in setting the knowledge agenda. But this promise raises an important question: is it realistic to imagine criminalised people as genuine decision-makers – equal partners in the production of criminal justice knowledge – *with the people and services explicitly holding power over them*? This is the central theme of this book.

We start by exploring understandings of *criminal justice knowledge* – what it is, who produces it, why, and for whom – and consider what makes the criminal justice context unique and distinct. We then trace the development of co-production as a concept and practice, identifying current understandings of its key elements and principles, which we distil into *participation*, *partnership*, and *power-sharing*.

What is criminal justice knowledge?

In posing the question of *what is criminal justice knowledge*, our underlying concern is firstly *what* is known, and secondly *how* this knowledge is produced, by whom, and according to whose logic and values. When speaking about the production of knowledge, we are thinking about the set of actions and actors involved in the process of making, manufacturing, or bringing forth knowledge and making it available for use. In the criminal justice context, these actions and actors are spread across the wide-reaching arms of the justice machinery. This system in fact comprises multiple systems – each encompassing legislation, institutions, personnel, policies, procedures, and practices – for dealing with victims of crime and "offenders" (a binary frequently shown to be blurry). These include police, courts, lawyers, judicial decision-makers, prisons, detention centres, community corrections, youth justice, and a range of other statutory or government agencies and personnel, as well as non-government and private organisations, funded and unfunded, that service the system and the people involved in it. What we "know" about criminal justice is generated by this vast array of actors and activities, each inputting and extracting information according to their needs, agendas, and priorities. However, as we examine next, not all needs, agendas, and priorities are given equal space or weight in the dominant discourses that shape contemporary criminal justice knowledge.

What counts as "evidence"?

The past four decades have seen a proliferation of criminal justice knowledge production aligned with the ascendancy of the *what works* agenda, predominant in the United States, the United Kingdom, Canada, and Australia. At its inception, this movement was a rejoinder to and repudiation of the 1970s "nothing works" edict and its political legacy. It focused on expounding effective practice or what does work in offender rehabilitation (Stout, 2017; Raynor, 2003). The emergence of *what works* as a dominant paradigm in correctional practice coincided with the rise of the biomedical model of evidence-based policy/practice (EBP), which tends to reflect a positivist or post-positivist understanding of the world. Correspondingly, knowledge in the context of criminal justice is often produced in the form of population-based, statistical information, with experimental study designs as the preferred means for evaluating what works.

These converging currents have coalesced into evidence-generating processes that reinforce and naturalise their own logic, methods, and assumptions, including the *hierarchy of evidence* (e.g. Doleac, 2019; cf. Glasby & Beresford, 2006). According to this schema, evidence of the impact or effectiveness of interventions is ranked: meta-analyses, systematic reviews, and experimental studies are classified as "gold standard"; while subjective or experiential insights are implicitly devalued as biased, "unscientific" (Glasby, 2011). Importantly, gold standard evaluative approaches to knowledge production privilege cause–effect explanations grounded in empirically testable variables, which tends to foreground individual factors and essentially ignore structural or contextual issues (Barry 2013).

We return in greater detail to this point – about hierarchy and ways of knowing – in the next chapter. For now, we argue that, rather than being static and fixed, conceptions of knowledge are in fact partial, contingent, and "constantly evolving" (Thyer, 2004: 168). One form of knowledge conceals, overlays, complements, and sits alongside other forms of knowledge and other perspectives. This observation about knowledge as partial and limited is, of course, not new. Many early writers highlighted the shortcomings of evidence-based decision-making, and EBP is now understood to denote the combination of research evidence, clinical or practitioner expertise, and lived experience (Glasby *et al.* 2007; Rubin & Parrish, 2007). In criminal justice, growing acknowledgement that "subjective perceptions are crucial in understanding the success or failure of correctional practice" (Maruna & LeBel, 2003: 93) has meant increasing incorporation of different sources of knowledge. The idea of integrating "subjective perceptions" in criminal justice policy or practice, however, highlights a crucial tension between competing rationales: *whose* knowledge is valued, and why?

The actuarial logics of criminal justice

What is "known" about criminal justice – its processes, practices, systems, subjects, and outcomes – has been heavily influenced and shaped by shifting modes of regulation and governance over recent decades. This shift incorporates the decline of penal-welfarism in Anglophone democracies (Garland, 2001), and the rise of so-called "new" practices and features of the criminal justice landscape: the new penology (Feeley & Simon, 1992), a new regulatory state (Crawford, 2009), the new punitiveness (Pratt *et al.* 2011), all framed by neoliberalism (Wacquant, 2010) ("neo-" meaning *new*). The various unfolding effects of this shift away from a welfare state and towards managerial, technocratic systems of justice and welfare "service delivery" are well established in criminological and social work scholarship and do not require full rehearsal here (see, for example, Garland, 2001; O'Malley, 2002; Stout, 2017). Suffice to note the emergence of a whole set of new practices and rationalities framed by neoliberal political, economic, and social values, including individualism, consumerism, personal responsibility, and choice. This has informed the replacement of traditional rehabilitative or punitive goals in criminal justice with *classifying* and *managing* groups of "offenders" in pursuit of administrative convenience, managerial efficiency, and effectiveness.

For the purposes of this book, we focus attention on two seemingly divergent aspects of the "rise of the new", which shape the conditions for criminal justice knowledge production, including co-production. First, *responsibilising failure*, how the State has disavowed and externalised responsibility for particular kinds of needs or problems in the lives of justice-involved people; second, the *commodification of justice* and its so-called consumers. These developments shape *what counts* as knowledge in criminal justice settings: what is deemed *knowable*, *necessary*, and *worth knowing*.

Responsibilising failure – the undeserving offender

Three decades ago, Feeley and Simon (1992) described as "the new penology" a shift from the rehabilitative ideal to the practices of actuarial justice. Contemporary criminal justice has reoriented away from the specific circumstances of individual lives and towards the aggregated tendencies of groups. What matters most is the capacity of the criminal justice system to consistently, efficiently, and effectively manage *criminal populations*, whose individual-level composition may fluctuate, but whose presence within society is seen as a given. In practice, this means that the support and equity needs of justice-involved people are reinterpreted and recalibrated through the narrow filters of risk and risk management. The focus is on estimating, classifying, preventing, and reducing the risk of future offending behaviour, in individual terms, rather than understanding or attending to broader societal conditions or underlying causal factors. Accordingly, what is deemed to be a "need" in contemporary criminal justice is something that is both "known" at a population level to correlate with recidivism and perceived to be "intervenable" in terms of individual risk reduction; systemic problems are recast as personal inadequacy (Hannah-Moffat, 2005; Maurutto & Hannah-Moffat, 2006).

So, what does this mean for producing criminal justice knowledge? Although increasingly detailed knowledge is being produced about *what works* to reduce recidivism, little attention is given to the insights and expertise of justice-involved people and their perspectives and experiences of the criminal justice system (Stout, 2017). Resurgent rhetoric about deserving/undeserving citizens, as Green and Rutherford (2000: 7) note, characterises "the visible and 'noisy' poor, disenfranchised working-class youth … [and] drug traffickers" as threats to community safety; "others" undeserving of help or understanding, yet deserving of harsh responses. Correspondingly, the knowledge that criminalised groups hold through their lived experience is not seen as *worth* knowing. In invoking the notion of socially disposable, "throwaway people" (Cahn, 2000), Cameron (2019) highlights a distinguishing feature of co-production in criminal justice contexts. Namely, it involves the rhetorically "undeserving", that is, people who have *done wrong*, people who some may consider *are* wrong (the "you're a wrongun" attitude[5]), and who have thereby forfeited their right to have a say in or about the justice responses to which they are subjected. More than just marginalised voices, these perspectives are considered unworthy, undeserving of wider attention.

Commodifying justice – the rights-bearing consumer

Narratives of individual responsibility are part of the wider marketisation and commodification of social services whereby "care" as a tradeable product arguably supplants human relational values (Davidson, 2015). Justice services are similarly commodified with "offenders" viewed "as 'portable entities' to be assessed and then 'managed into' appropriate resources" (Robinson, 2005: 310). The notion of "consumer choice", drawn from neo-classical economic theory, underlies competitive managerial policies and practices such as privatisation and marketisation in public service delivery. Its central tenet is that people have the right to choose or make decisions about services provided to them (Healy, 2014). The terms *consumer, client, service user*, or *customer* suggest "empowered citizens" (Hall *et al.* 2003), able to demand, purchase, and choose services of a certain type and standard. However, "consumers" of correctional services are "*involuntary* clients" (Trotter, 2015) compelled by way of a court order or threat of legal penalty to use services that they may experience as intrusive or controlling. For these reasons, Weaver notes (2011, p.1040), "offenders cannot un-problematically be cast as consumers".

"Consumer choice" ideology is core to broader consumer and citizens' rights movements, viewed as a vehicle for promoting individual self-determination and the personalisation of services (Healy, 2014). It helped drive deinstitutionalisation policies in mental health and child welfare during the 1970s and, more recently, "consumer-directed care" in ageing and disability support services (Healy, 2014). These policy shifts are also premised on *rational choice theory*, one of several microeconomic theories about consumer choice that, since the 1980s, has become popular in criminal justice. Rational choice holds that people "choose" to commit offences based on reasoned cost–benefit analysis (Barry, 2013). Thus, as De'Ath *et al.* (2018: 87) observe, offending is "framed as an individual's 'bad choice' ... requiring punishment"; a "voluntaristic conception of crime, which locates the reasons for crime within the social actor" (Cunneen *et al.* 2015: 26). Though designating people subject to involuntary mental health or disability "treatment" as "consumers" may be similarly problematic, in contrast to the lived experience of people deemed unwell or disabled through no "fault" of their own, criminalised people's lived experience is always framed by these normative assumptions about crime. People are cast as justice system "consumers" because of their "poor choices" yet simultaneously deemed unworthy to be heard. Clearly, this limits people's capacity to participate or collaborate in interventions, including co-production.

What *is* co-production?

Co-production is "a slippery concept" (SCIE, 2015), variously conceptualised, and practised, and often ambiguously defined. The simple definition we opened with – "equal partnership and for equal benefit" – while pithy and practical, immediately raises questions: who is in partnership, on whose terms, for whose benefit, and "equal" by whose measure? The earliest formulation of co-production referred to citizens' active participation in the provision of public goods and services, to improve quality and/or quantity of services, thereby reducing costs to the State[6] (Ostrom *et al.* 1978; Kiser & Percy, 1980; Brudney & England, 1983). Growing alongside the civil rights movements of the 1960s and 1970s, citizen participation also represented a site of struggle between powerholders and the powerless and a push towards emancipation and transformation. Arnstein's (1969) "Ladder of Citizen Participation" articulates a deliberately provocative typology of "citizen power", ranging from empty tokenism to full citizen control. Her ultimate aim, though, is "the redistribution of power that enables the have-not citizens, presently excluded from the political and economic process, to be deliberately included in the future" (1969: 216). Co-production thus fundamentally entails *active participation*.

These categories still resonate through co-production practices and conceptualisations. For instance, Hanley *et al.*'s (2004) simplified continuum of consultation, collaboration, and user control is useful, but fails to account for illusory or "sham" participation (McLaughlin, 2006: 1397). Slay and Stephens (2013: 4) distil Arnstein's ladder into doing *to*, doing *for,* and doing *with*; co-production means "doing with" and "shifts power towards people". Roper, Grey and Cadogan (2018: 5), in outlining co-production principles and practices in mental health, differentiate co-production from other forms of participation in that it:

> deliberately sets out to create a culture that values all expertise and knowledge, particularly the expertise and knowledge of the people that are most affected by the problem and solution. Co-production recognises and seeks to address power differentials within partnerships.

Arnstein (1969: 216) cautioned, further,

> that participation without redistribution of power is an empty and frustrating process for the powerless. It allows the powerholders to claim that all sides were considered, but makes it possible for only some of those sides to benefit. It maintains the status quo.

If co-production is indeed differentiated by the recognition of – and attempt to balance – unequal power relations, does this always imply a challenge to the status quo? How does this fit within a system, such as justice, designed to preserve social control and legal order? We return to Arnstein's ladder, and to consider her warning, further below.

Understandings and definitions of co-production have been emerging and changing rapidly over the last decade. The shift from participation and collaboration to co-planning, co-design, co-delivery, and co-evaluation in research and practice, and even "co-governance" or "co-management" (Verschuere *et al.* 2012), signals this developing thinking. Arguably, however, co-production has been used so ubiquitously as to become a buzzword, risking the loss of its radical roots and disguising a wide diversity of practices, motives, and rationales (Cameron, 2019; Sorrentino *et al.* 2018). This ubiquity leads to what Williams and colleagues (2020:.2) term "cobiquity", which:

> disregards significant differences between collaborative traditions, such as who is involved, how they are involved, the experiences people bring, and to what extent such processes address structural and interpersonal inequalities in power.

The issue of unequal power (explored in the next chapter) is a recurring motif throughout this book.

A snapshot of the co-production literature

The international co-production literature, and its associated "plethora of 'co' words" (Williams *et al.* 2020: 2), crosses many disciplines spanning public sector innovation and service delivery.[7] The last decade has seen a rapid interest in co-production, in the context of "pervasive political discourse on user involvement and community participation that has reconfigured organisational set-ups managing different kinds of welfare services" (Kirkegaard & Andersen 2018: 829). Part of this discourse includes the notions of citizens' rights and consumer choice, discussed earlier, which developed alongside co-production concepts from fields such as mental health, alcohol and other drug treatment, youth work, and disability. Perhaps unsurprisingly, the co-production literature is most well-developed in settings where service users are more easily cast as "consumers". Recognising that the boundaries of these systems intersect with one another, and with criminal justice, we draw from this literature to guide our understanding.

Most of the co-production literature originates from the United Kingdom, where service user involvement has been embedded in health policy development since the 1990s. Smith *et al.* (2012 in De'Ath *et al.* 2018) tie these developments to the New Labour agenda of the time, which drove public sector reforms and a focus on efficiency and accountability. The resultant attention to "customer" feedback and satisfaction is clear evidence of managerialism as one of its origins. The UK Care Act 2014 was one of the first pieces of legislation to specifically include the concept of co-production in its statutory guidance. A myriad of online practice and policy resources illustrate the extent to which co-production has unmistakably "arrived in the UK" (Boyle & Harris, 2009: 3): for example, the London-based Social Care Institute for Excellence (SCIE) has a long history of leading co-production initiatives, providing training and resources and hosting a national co-production network; England's Local Government Association provides guidance on co-production for over 300 councils; the National Health Service (NHS) provides resources for health services across England and Wales; *All in this together* (Pawb gyda'i gilydd) is the Co-production Network for Wales; the Scottish Co-production Network hosts an annual co-production week in Scotland; and the Co-production Collective (based at University College London) works with universities, charities, funders, and community groups.

In terms of leading agencies, Nesta and the New Economics Foundation have published seminal reports, including Slay and Stephens's (2013) *Co-production in Mental Health: A Literature Review* and Nesta's (2012) *People Powered Health Co-Production Catalogue.* These identify core tenets of co-production:

- **Taking an assets-based approach** – recognising people as assets, seeing them as active citizens and equal partners, rather than passive recipients;
- **Building on people's existing capabilities** – moving from a deficit-based approach, towards supporting people to work with and develop their strengths;
- **Reciprocity and mutuality** – developing two-way, reciprocal relationships for people to work together with mutual responsibilities and expectations;
- **Peer support networks** – encouraging peer support and personal networks, alongside professionals, as the best way of transferring knowledge;
- **Blurring distinctions or roles** – removing tightly defined boundaries between professionals and recipients to enable shared responsibility and control;
- **Facilitating rather than delivering** – service agencies becoming catalysts and facilitators of change rather than providing or delivering all the services themselves; "supporting things to happen and catalysing other action" (Nesta, 2012: 7).

Despite overlaps with other approaches – including, among others, participatory research, asset-based community development,[8] or anti-oppressive practice[9] – co-production requires *all* these principles to be embedded in practice, albeit to varying degrees (Nesta, 2012; Slay & Stephens, 2013). These principles run through much of the co-production literature.

Identifying criminal justice co-production

Loeffler and Bovaird (2020) summarise current though "relatively undeveloped" (p.208) evidence on co-production in criminal justice. They observe that much of the international justice-related co-production literature refers to "co-delivery through citizen action",[10] while elements such as "co-commissioning, co-design and co-assessment" remain relatively rare (p.209). As Herrick and Bauer (2020) observe, in the United States, "[w]hile the idea of co-creation in government isn't new, it's still far from the status quo". This seems due, at least in significant part, to ambiguity about what sort of activities constitute co-production, that is, what co-production actually *is*.

In New Zealand, for instance, Thom and Burnside (2018) identified five studies[11] focused on the fit between co-production and "the contested site of rehabilitation in criminal justice" (p.1260). Most demonstrated "individualized forms of co-production that lead to individual outcomes", including personal support for desistance (p.1260). Yet – especially when these practices remain invisible as "hidden experimentation" (Surva *et al.* 2016: 1040), thereby effecting limited systemic change – it is difficult to discern how, exactly, co-production varies from any kind of strengths-based relational or emancipatory intervention. Thom and Burnside thus highlight how many practices described as co-production might often more accurately fall under "different approaches to personalised[12] offender management" (Fox *et al.* 2018). They also show how challenging it is to identify a body of research and practice knowledge that squarely fits under the heading of *criminal justice co-production*.

Scotland's Beth Weaver and colleagues have led the way in academic and practitioner-focused work on criminal justice co-production,[13] defining it as "a participatory and collaborative approach between citizen-consumers of services, policy-makers and professionals to the design, delivery and evaluation of criminal justice" (Weaver & McCulloch 2012: 4). Differentiating *individualistic, group*, and *collective* forms of co-production in community justice (Weaver & McCulloch, 2012; Weaver *et al.* 2019), they see *individual* co-production as the dominant strategy currently used and aligned with person-centred support (congruent with Thom and Burnside's NZ review). Approaches to *group* co-production, such as peer support groups, typically involve service users coming together to shape or provide services that benefit the group's members, whereas *collective* forms of co-production go beyond this to benefit the wider community, such as through co-design and delivery of services. It is argued that co-production should *include* but cannot be reduced to service user design, involvement, or consultation; that "the whole is greater than the sum of its parts" (Nesta, 2012: 5). Weaver, Lightowler, and Moodie (2019), however, note that the term co-production is not well-recognised or widely used in criminal justice, in comparison to the term user involvement, concluding "However you label what you do ... *why* you do it, *what* you actually do, *how* you do it, and *who with* is arguably more important" (p.7, our emphasis).

Irrespective of definitional challenges, criminal justice co-production has become established in the United Kingdom over the past decade through the work of a range of third sector organisations (see, for example, User Voice, 2010; Clinks, 2011; Revolving Doors, 2016), and smaller grassroots initiatives such as the Hidden Voices Project, a collaboration between imprisoned poets and Twitter users, led by Glasgow-based First Time Inside.[14] Drawing on Clinks (2016) *Guide to service user involvement and co-production*, Weaver *et al.* (2019: 11) usefully outline the range of activities that service user involvement (or co-production) can encompass, and what each can entail, as "a continuum of opportunities for participation" (see Figure 1.1). Beyond outlining the range of activities that provide "different opportunities for people to have their say and to different ends", according to people's "different interests, skills and strengths" (Weaver *et al.* 2019: 11), this is useful insofar as it complicates simple definitions and shows that co-production is a continuum, *not one thing*. It shows how co-production has emerged – and continues to emerge – from "a rich, diverse and contested lineage of theory and experimentation" (Durose & Richardson, 2016: 33).

In Australia, criminal justice co-production is not so widely or well established. But in alcohol and other drug treatment, disability, and mental health (De'Ath *et al.* 2018), co-production is becoming routinely embedded into policy and clinical guidelines as a key principle for person-centred practice. Of particular influence is Roper *et al.*'s (2018) report, *Co-production: Putting principles into practice in mental health contexts*, which offers thoughtful critique and advice that is applicable in criminal justice contexts too. Indeed, intersecting justice sectors, such as family violence, youth justice,[15] and forensic mental health have recently begun to engage "experts by experience" in the design and evaluation of research, services, and policy. In contrast, beyond emerging references to the importance of lived experience,[16] scholarly work on co-production in criminal justice in Australia remains scarce (De'Ath *et al.* 2018).

Fundamental principles: participation, partnership, power-sharing

Despite the variations noted, common and consistent themes are evident across the co-production literature: seeing people as assets; building on

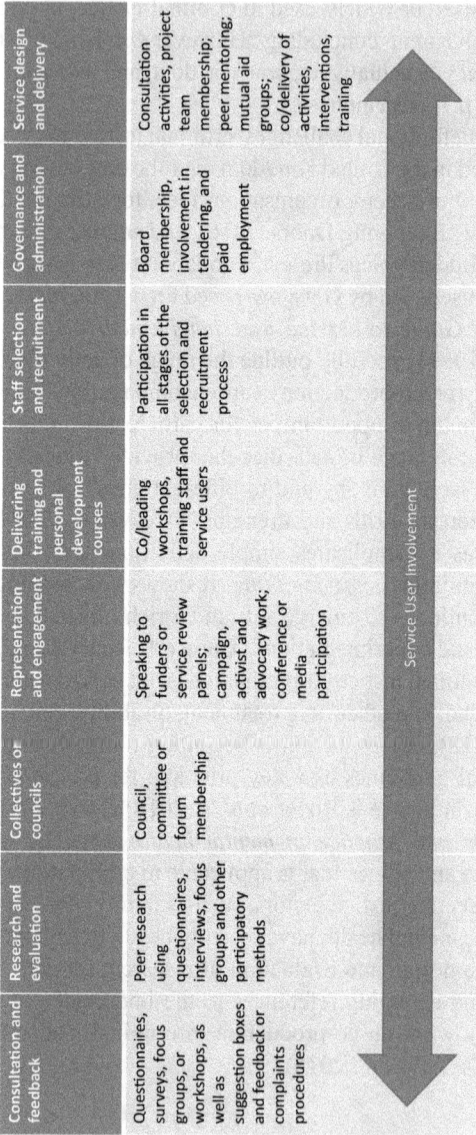

Consultation and feedback	Research and evaluation	Collectives or councils	Representation and engagement	Delivering training and personal development courses	Staff selection and recruitment	Governance and administration	Service design and delivery
Questionnaires, surveys, focus groups, or workshops, as well as suggestion boxes and feedback or complaints procedures	Peer research using questionnaires, interviews, focus groups and other participatory methods	Council, committee or forum membership	Speaking to funders or service review panels; campaign, activist and advocacy work; conference or media participation	Co/leading workshops, training staff and service users	Participation in all stages of the selection and recruitment process	Board membership, involvement in tendering, and paid employment	Consultation activities, project team membership; peer mentoring; mutual aid groups; co/delivery of activities, interventions, training

Service User Involvement

Figure 1.1 A continuum of opportunities for participation (adapted from Weaver et al. 2019: 11).

people's capabilities; reciprocity and mutuality; networks; blurring roles; and services as facilitators and catalysts (Boyle *et al.* 2010; Nesta, 2012; Slay & Stephens, 2013). Roper *et al.* (2018: 6) condense these into guiding tenets for mental health: "consumers" as partners from the outset; acknowledgement and addressing of power differentials; and the development of "consumer" leadership and capacity. In translating and applying these ideas to criminal justice, we find it useful to distil three fundamental and interrelated principles: *participation*, *partnership*, and *power-sharing*. These ideas are central to the questions at the heart of this book: What or who makes the "co" in co-production? And what makes co-production in and about criminal justice distinct from co-production in other contexts?

As indicated, co-production fundamentally entails *active participation*. Roper *et al.* (2018: 2) highlight both role type and timing in the demand for *early and ongoing* participation in mental health, emphasising that:

> co-production raises the bar ... shifting from seeking *involvement or participation* **after** an agenda has already been set, to seeking consumer *leadership* **from the outset**.
>
> (original emphasis)

Yet in criminal justice, where "othering" is more persistent, this may not always be realistic. As one formerly imprisoned person ("C" quoted in McCulloch 2016: 439-440) explains, in prison, "you are on the bottom rung ... the purpose of the sentence is to put you in your place, as an offender". Others worry that co-production in the criminal justice system risks being another "top-down, tick box process" (McCulloch, 2016: 440). Acknowledging these risks, formerly imprisoned Paula (2021) emphasises that genuine co-production demands "equity and equality; where ... cooperation and collective responsibility exist, or are, at the very least, a destination". Equal partnership, then, is an ideal of participation that is certainly not guaranteed.

Rose and Kalathil (2019: 8), in the context of mental health, point out that projects that may look like partnerships often *hide*, rather than abolish, "persistent power relations based on both status and knowledge possession". The question of *who gets to partner* is pivotal in criminal justice. For instance, McCulloch and Members of *Positive Prison? Positive Futures* ... (2016) reported that "only those offenders with pro-social identity and access to resources to a certain level were able to succeed in co-production", citing "class issues" as central (in Thom & Burnside, 2018: 1260). Beyond class, this has clear implications for genuine partnerships if we consider the disproportionate levels of trauma and marginalisation among criminalised populations. The promise of co-production in opening up new "generative terrain" between professional knowledge and lived experience expertise cannot be realised as long as inherited hierarchies of power and difference persist (Rose & Kalathil, 2019: 2). This applies equally, perhaps even more starkly, in criminal justice settings, where "power protectionism" (Paula, 2021) is built into every interaction. Without interrogating power as a fundamental issue to be addressed, or challenging underlying assumptions about deserving and "undeserving" citizens, co-production risks becoming a "supermarketized vision of service user involvement" (Cowden & Singh, 2007: 6).

Summing up co-production so far

In simple terms, co-production ideally involves working–making–doing together, disrupting power relations and traditional hierarchies, producing knowledge, and improving service provision through discussion with those who experience it. But it is no easy task to get powerholders to recalibrate their practices to work–make–do together with those using or otherwise affected by services, or to effect substantial structural and attitudinal changes. Nor is there any guarantee that what is produced will be regarded as co-production. For many, the widespread adoption and diversity of co-production practices in human services suggest that it has been co-opted and diluted, reducing a "truly radical and potentially powerful" concept, which has the potential to disrupt power relations and traditional hierarchies, to a "buzzword ... rebadging ... service user involvement" (Cameron, 2019), which brings us back to the question: how realistic is it to imagine criminal justice "service users" as not only participants, but also decision-makers or equal partners in the production of criminal justice knowledge with the services and professionals who hold power over them, and by whom they are (potentially) coerced, contained, and punished?

Structure of the book

This book is in three parts: Part I explores the concept of co-production, its application in criminal justice, and key theoretical undercurrents; Part II presents case studies to show what co-production can look like in various justice-related settings; and Part III draws out tensions, paradoxes, and possibilities of co-producing knowledge in these contexts.

Part I: In this opening chapter, we have raised many complexities that inevitably arise in efforts to co-produce knowledge in and about criminal justice. To try and explain the challenges and limits of co-production – and its transformative or emancipatory potential – we need some tools for *thinking with*. In Chapter 2, therefore, we outline a conceptual framework comprising *power and hierarchy* and *ways of knowing*. These ideas are present in so much of what is written about co-production – often implicitly, sometimes overtly – that we think they are important to bring to the surface. We use these concepts in our analysis of the case studies presented in the second part of the book.

Part II: In Chapters 3–6, we use case studies to delve into particular examples of what people *do* when they co-produce knowledge in/about criminal justice. We present examples – not exhaustive, but illustrative – of co-production across different sites and settings: in prisons; with criminalised women; from practitioners' perspectives; and with First Nations communities. The case studies exemplify different issues, approaches, principles, and practices, including some that might be identified beyond the co-production label. In this way, we reveal some of the complexities that arise in trying to pin down this multiform concept.

Part III: In Chapters 7 and 8, we apply our conceptual lenses of power, hierarchy, and ways of knowing to critically analyse the different examples of co-production the case studies offer. Chapter 7 reveals themes of time, space, and identity in making sense of the limits of co-production within/ against the rigid realities of criminal justice. In Chapter 8, we reflect on what or who makes the "co" in co-production, identify the distinguishing features of co-producing knowledge in and about criminal justice, and consider the potential of co-production to bring about genuine change.

Notes

1 https://www.coproductioncollective.co.uk/what- is-co-production/our-approach.
2 We use the hyphenated version to acknowledge that this term is still emerging, still variously conceptualised and defined, and not widely understood outside academic and practice circles.
3 While many scholars prefer to use "knowledges" (as in Donna Haraway's 1988 "Situated Knowledges") to capture and signify the plural and contested nature of what is known and knowable and different ways of knowing, we acknowledge and assume this multiplicity – and its ontological, epistemological, ethical, and political implications – in our use of the singular form "knowledge".
4 In this book, we refer to the Sovereign First Peoples of Australia as Aboriginal and Torres Strait Islander, Indigenous, or First Nations peoples.
5 Quote from a User Voice council member – see https://www.uservoice.org/work -with-us/
6 This conceptualisation of co-production includes a diverse array of public services, from policing (Percy, 1978) to postal services (Alford, 2009). This version of co-production is emblematic of the "new public management" paradigm of the 1980s, embodying free-market principles of costs/benefits and efficiency and government withdrawal from public service delivery.
7 See, for example, Voorberg *et al.*'s (2015) review of literature between 1987 and 2013 on co-production and the associated concept of co-creation.

8 See Mathie & Cunningham (2003) for an overview of asset-based community development.
9 See Wilson & Beresford's (2000) account of Anti-Oppressive Practice from social service users' perspectives.
10 We do not describe responsibilising community policing practices, such as where citizens participate in crime prevention, as co-production (e.g. Meijer, 2014).
11 The five studies they cite are: Fox et al. 2013; McCulloch with Members of Positive Prison? Positive Futures..., 2016; Surva et al. 2016; Weaver, 2011; Weaver & McNeill, 2011.
12 Weaver (2011:1042) and Fox *et al.* (2018:35) suggest co-production is a "deeper" approach to personalisation. "Personalisation" appears in the co-production literature, predominantly in connection to the United Kingdom social care sector, and refers to tailoring services to meet the needs and preferences of individual citizens.
13 See, for example: Weaver, 2011; Weaver & Lightowler, 2012; Weaver & McCulloch, 2012; Weaver & Nicholson, 2012; Weaver, Moodie & Lightowler, 2017; Weaver, Lightowler & Moodie, 2019.
14 This project led to the 2020 publication of the co-produced "Saughton Sonnets" anthology: see https://firsttimeinside.co.uk/hidden-voices/
15 See for example Domestic Violence Victoria's (2020) The Family Violence Experts by Experience Framework. Also in Australia, several services connected directly or indirectly to the youth justice system have established advisory bodies whose membership comprises young people.
16 See for example: Hall, 2017; Armstrong, 2020; Schwartz *et al.* 2020; Sotiri, 2020; DEDICA-20, 2021; Doyle *et al.* 2021.

References

Alford, J (2009) *Engaging public sector clients*. London: Palgrave Macmillan.
Arnstein, S (1969) A ladder of citizen participation, *Journal of the American Institute of Planners*, 35(4): 216–224.
Anthony, T & Baldry, E (2017) FactCheck Q&A: Are Indigenous Australians the most incarcerated people on Earth? *The Conversation*, June 6.
Barry, M (2013) Rational choice and responsibilisation in youth justice in Scotland: Whose evidence matters in evidence-based policy? *Howard Journal of Criminal Justice*, 52(4): 347–364.
Brudney, J & England, R (1983) Toward a definition of the coproduction concept, *Public Administration Review*, 43(1): 59–65.
Boyle, D & Harris, M (2009) *The challenge of co-production: How equal partnerships between professionals and the public are crucial to improving public services*. London: New Economics Foundation & Nesta.
Boyle, D, Slay, L & Stephens, L (2010) *Public services inside out: Putting co-production into practice*. London: New Economics Foundation & Nesta.
Cahn, E (2000) *No more throwaway people: The co-production imperative*. Washington, DC: Essential Books.
Cameron, A (2019) Co-production – Radical Roots, Radical Results, blog post, November 10. https://allywritesblog.wordpress.com/2019/11/10/co-production-radical-roots-radical-results/

Clinks (2011) *A Review of service user involvement in prisons and probation trusts.* London: Clinks.

Clinks (2016) *Service user involvement and co-production.* London: Clinks.

Cowden, S & Singh, G (2007) The 'user': Friend, foe or fetish? A critical exploration of user involvement in health and social care, *Critical Social Policy*, 27(1): 5–23.

Crawford, A (2009) Governing through anti-social behaviour: Regulatory challenges to criminal justice, *British Journal of Criminology*, 49(6): 810–831.

Cunneen, C, White, R & Richards, K (2015) *Juvenile justice: Youth and crime in Australia*, 5th ed. South Melbourne: Oxford University Press.

Davidson, B (2015) Community aged care providers in a competitive environment: Past, present and future. In G Meagher & S Goodwin (Eds.), *Markets, rights and power in Australian social policy*. Sydney: Sydney University Press, pp. 191–229.

De'Ath, S, Flynn, C & Field-Pimm, M (2018) Building knowledge of consumer participation in criminal justice in Australia: A case study, *International Journal for Crime, Justice & Social Democracy* 7(1): 76–90.

DEDICA-20 (2021) COVID-19, crisis and imagination, *Current Issues in Criminal Justice*, 33(1): 144–149.

Doleac, J (2019) "Evidence-based policy" should reflect a hierarchy of evidence, *Journal of Policy Analysis & Management*, 38(2): 517–519.

Domestic Violence Victoria (2020) *The Family Violence Experts by Experience Framework Report.* Melbourne: Domestic Violence Victoria.

Doyle, C, Gardner, K & Wells, K (2021) The importance of incorporating lived experience in efforts to reduce Australian reincarceration rates, *International Journal for Crime, Justice & Social Democracy*, 10(2): 83–98.

Durose, C & Richardson, L (2016) *Designing public policy for co-production: Theory, practice and change.* Bristol: Policy Press.

Feeley, M & Simon, J (1992) The new penology: Notes on the emerging strategy of corrections and its implications, *Criminology*, 30(4): 449–474.

Fox, C, Harrison, J, Marsh, C & Smith, A (2018) Piloting different approaches to personalised offender management in the English criminal justice system, *International Review of Sociology*, 28(1): 35–61.

Garland, D (2001) *The culture of control.* Oxford: Oxford University Press.

Glasby, J (2011) From evidence-based to knowledge-based policy and practice. In J. Glasby (Ed.), *Evidence, policy and practice: Critical perspectives in health and social care*. Bristol: Policy Press, pp. 85–98.

Glasby, J & Beresford, P (2006) Who knows best? Evidence-based practice and the service user contribution, *Critical Social Policy*, 26(1): 268–284.

Glasby, J, Walshe, K & Harvey, G (Eds.). (2007) Evidence-based practice, *Evidence and Policy, Special Issue*, 3(3): 323–457.

Green, P & Rutherford, A (Eds.). (2000) *Criminal policy in transition.* Oxford/ Portland: Hart Publishing.

Hall, C, Juhila, K, Parton, N & Poso, T (2003) *Constructing clienthood in social work and human services: Interaction, identities and practices.* London: Jessica Kingsley Publishers.

Hall, M (2017) *The lived sentence: Rethinking sentencing, risk and rehabilitation.* London: Palgrave Macmillan, Springer.

Hanley, B, Bradburn, J, Barnes, M, Evans, C, Goodare, H, Kelson, M, Kent, A, Oliver, S, Thomas, S & Wallcraft, J (2004) *Involving the public in NHS, public health and social care: Briefing notes for researchers*. Eastleigh: Involve.

Hannah-Moffatt, K (2005) Criminogenic needs and the transformative risk subject: Hybridizations of risk/need in penality, *Punishment & Society*, 7(1): 29–51.

Healy, K (2014) *Social work theories in context: Creating frameworks for practice*, 2nd edn. London: Macmillan Education.

Herrick, E & Bauer, C (2020) Toward co-designing a better criminal justice system, *Stanford Social Innovation Review*, June 26. https://ssir.org/articles/entry/toward_co_designing_a_better_criminal_justice_system

Kirkegaard, S & Andersen, D (2018) Co-production in community mental health services: Blurred boundaries or a game of pretend? *Sociology of Health & Illness*, 40(5): 828–842.

Kiser, LL & Percy, SL (1980) The concept of coproduction and its implications for public service delivery. Presented at the annual meeting of the American Society for Public Administration, San Francisco, April 13-16. https://dlc.dlib.indiana.edu

Loeffler, E & Bovaird, T (2020) Assessing the impact of co-production on pathways to outcomes in public services: The case of policing and criminal justice, *International Public Management Journal*, 23(2): 205–223.

Maruna, S & LeBel, T (2003) Welcome home? Examining the "reentry court" concept from a strengths-based perspective, *Western Criminology Review*, 4(2): 91–107.

Mathie, A & Cunningham, G (2003) From clients to citizens: Asset-based community development as a strategy for community-driven development, *Development in Practice*, 13(5): 474–486.

Maurutto, P & Hannah-Moffat, K (2006) Assembling risk and the restructuring of penal control, *British Journal of Criminology*, 46(3): 438–454.

McCulloch, T with Members of Positive Prison? Positive Futures (2016) Co-producing justice sanctions? Citizen perspectives, *Criminology & Criminal Justice*, 16(4): 431–451.

McLaughlin, H (2006) Involving young service users as co-researchers: Possibilities, benefits and costs, *British Journal of Social Work*, 36(8): 1395–1410.

Nesta (2012) *People powered health co-production catalogue*. London: Nesta.

O'Malley, P (2002) Globalising risk? Distinguishing styles of 'neo-liberal' criminal justice in Australia and the USA, *Criminology & Criminal Justice*, 2(2): 205–222.

Ostrom, E, Parks, RB, Whitaker, GP & Percy, SL (1978) The public service production process: A framework for analyzing police services, *Policy Studies Journal*, 7(1): 381–389.

Paula (2021) Thoughts from Paula. In *Prison: A place for co-production*, UCL Public Engagement Blog, January 18. https://blogs.ucl.ac.uk/public-engagement/2021/01/18/prison-a-place-for-co-production/

Percy, SL (1978) Conceptualizing and measuring citizen co-production of community safety, *Policy Studies Journal*, 7: 486–493.

Pratt, J, Brown, D, Brown, M, Hallsworth, S & Morrison, W (2011) *The new punitiveness*. Oxon: Routledge.

Raynor, P (2003) Research in probation: From 'nothing works' to 'what works'. In WH Chui & M Nellis (Eds.), *Moving probation forward: Evidence, arguments and practice*. Essex: Pearson Education Limited, pp. 74–91.

Revolving Doors (2016) *Service user involvement with offenders in the community: A toolkit for staff*. London: Revolving Doors Agency.

Robinson, G (2005) What works in offender management? *Howard Journal of Criminal Justice*, 44(3): 307–318.

Roper, C, Grey, F & Cadogan, E (2018) *Co-production: Putting principles into practice in mental health contexts*. Melbourne: School of Health Sciences, The University of Melbourne.

Rose, D & Kalathil, J (2019) Power, privilege and knowledge: The untenable promise of co-production in mental "health", *Hypothesis & Theory*, 4(57): 1–11.

Rubin, A & Parrish, D (2007) Views of evidence-based practice among faculty in master of social work programs: A national survey, *Research on Social Work Practice*, 17(1): 110–122.

Schwartz, M, Russell, S, Baldry, E, Brown, D, Cunneen, C & Stubbs, J (2020) *Obstacles to effective support of people released from prison: Wisdom from the field*. Rethinking Community Sanctions Project. Sydney: UNSW.

SCIE (2015) *Co-production in social care: What it is and how to do it*, SCIE Guide 51. London: Social Care Institute for Excellence.

Slay, J & Stephens, L (2013) *Co-production in mental health: A literature review*. London: New Economics Foundation.

Smith, M, Gallagher, M, Wosu, H, Stewart, J, Cree, V, Hunter, S, Evans, S, Montgomery, C, Holiday, S & Wilkinson, H (2012) Engaging with involuntary service users in social work: Findings from a knowledge exchange project, *British Journal of Social Work*, 42(8): 1460–1477.

Sorrentino, M, Sicilia, M & Howlett, M (2018) Understanding co-production as a new public governance tool, *Policy & Society*, 37(3): 277–293.

Sotiri, M (2020) Building pathways out of the justice system: Supporting women and reducing recidivism, *Precedent*, 161: 48–52.

Stout, B (2017) *Community justice in Australia: Developing knowledge, skills and values for working with offenders in the community*. Crows Nest: Allen & Unwin.

Surva, L, Tõnurist, P & Lember, V (2016) Co-production in a network setting: Providing an alternative to the national probation service, *International Journal of Public Administration*, 9(13): 1031–1043.

Thom, K & Burnside, D (2018) Sharing power in criminal justice: The potential of co-production for offenders experiencing mental health and addictions in New Zealand, *International Journal of Mental Health Nursing*, 27: 1258–1265.

Thyer, BA (2004) What is evidence-based practice? *Brief Treatment & Crisis Intervention*, 4(2): 167–176.

Trotter, C (2015) *Working with involuntary clients: A guide to practice*, 3rd edn. New York: Routledge.

User Voice (2010) *The power inside: The role of prison councils*. London: User Voice.

Verschuere, B, Brandsen, T & Pestoff, V (2012) Co-production: The state of the art in research and the future agenda, *Voluntas*, 23: 1083–1101.

Voorberg, WH, Bekkers, VJJM & Tummers, LG (2015) A systematic review of co-creation and co-production: Embarking on the social innovation journey, *Public Management Review*, 17(9): 1333–1357.

Wacquant, L (2010) Crafting the neoliberal state: Workfare, prisonfare, and social insecurity, *Sociological Forum*, 25(2): 197–220.

Weaver, B (2011) Co-producing community justice: The transformative potential of personalisation for penal sanctions, *British Journal of Social Work*, 41(6): 1038–1057.

Weaver, B & McCulloch, T (2012) Co-producing criminal justice: Executive summary. The Scottish Centre for Crime and Justice Research (SCCJR), Report No.05/2012.

Weaver, B, Lightowler, C & Moodie, K (2019) Inclusive justice: Co-producing change – A practical guide to service user involvement in community justice. CYCJ, Scotland.

Williams, O, Sarre, S, Papoulias, SC, Knowles, S, Robert, G, Beresford, P, Rose, D, Carr, S, Kaur, M & Palmer, VJ (2020) Lost in the shadows: Reflections on the dark side of co-production, *Health Research Policy & Systems*, 18(43): 1–10.

Wilson, A & Beresford, P (2000) 'Anti-oppressive practice': Emancipation or appropriation? *British Journal of Social Work*, 30(5): 553–573.

2 Power, hierarchy, and ways of knowing

Co-production is, on one level, straightforward: it involves working–making–doing together. But, as we've outlined, it is complicated by two realities: it is defined and practised in different ways; and in criminal justice, in particular, it is constrained by certain logics and rationales that shape relations at the micro- and macro-levels, between individuals and the systems and institutions in which they operate. These aspects of criminal justice[1] (the vast array of enmeshed actors, agencies, and activities outlined in Chapter 1) are infused with patterns, policies, and practices that over recent decades have appeared increasingly "dualistic, ambivalent, and often contradictory" (Garland, 1996: 446). On the one hand, perceived social, economic, and political threats have driven increasingly punitive and exclusionary government policies. On the other, demand for improved rehabilitative and reintegrative outcomes has burgeoned alongside the desire for more effective and efficient expenditure. And the drive to accumulate "evidence" to justify spending, and on which to base policy and practice decisions, has embedded the "science" of evaluation and measurement in much programme design.

This dualism and contradiction also pervade co-production discourse and practice. We see this in the way co-production is *not one thing*. It can comprise distinct yet often overlapping purposes and arrangements: co-production can be an approach to governance, to inform policy or make decisions about service design and delivery; it can be a process of generating new knowledge, perspectives, and insights through research, evaluation, or practice in the field; and it can provide a way of improving practice and programme or service delivery (which clearly overlaps with the first two). Its outcomes are varied too. At its worst, it risks being tokenistic, reinscribing relations of inferiority, and valorising existing criminal justice systems and structures. At its best, shared power and "equal and reciprocal relationships" (Slay & Stephens, 2013: 4) promise a radical shakeup of hegemonic ways of knowing and being in the world, in material

DOI: 10.4324/9780429328657-3

ways. This promise, in Australia, given our colonial history, must include bringing about Aboriginal and Torres Strait Islander peoples' genuine self-determination and the valuing of Indigenous knowledge alongside other forms of knowledge. The danger is that it simply reproduces and reinforces settler-colonial logic and practices.

This multiplicity provides a clue as to how we might think about the conceptual threads that are knotted together in the practices and promises of co-production. Central to all its different manifestations are the questions of power, hierarchy, and the subordination of knowledge, with the possibility of elevating different voices and perspectives. In this chapter, we set up a conceptual framework – a set of ideas – to help us think through and engage with these complexities, and to explore the possibilities and limitations of co-producing knowledge in and about criminal justice. These ideas are loosely gathered under the headings *power and hierarchy* and *ways of knowing*.

Power and hierarchy

We assume knowledge to be multiple and contested, yet it is commonly presented as monolithic: fixed, singular, and dominated by one way of knowing. For instance, when we talk about "criminal justice knowledge" – or what is "known" about the criminal justice system – it invokes a traditional hierarchical view of a relationship between the State and its citizens, which is largely uncontested. At the top of this hierarchy sits the State, which holds the power to punish its citizens, power that is invested in and exercised by a range of actors. The symbols that communicate this power are embedded and embodied in a range of ways: from courtroom and sentencing rituals to the uniforms and weapons worn and wielded by police and corrections officers. Many others occupy the middle echelons: social workers, psychologists, caseworkers, for instance, all those involved in the administering or scrutiny of criminal justice. At the bottom of the hierarchy are people convicted of criminal offences, those subjected to the penal power of the State and tarnished by the enduring stigma of being an "offender".

Definitions of co-production (discussed in Chapter 1) both build on and disrupt notions of hierarchy: from Arnstein's (1969) ladder of citizen power, ranging from empty ritual to citizen control; to Slay and Stephens' (2013) alternative ladder of *doing to*, *doing for*, and *doing with*. These typologies are deliberately simplified for the sake of abstraction, of course, but they are useful to illustrate caste dynamics between those with power and those without (notwithstanding differences among them). Yet their categories reveal nothing of the obstacles to participation, such as "powerholders' ... racism, paternalism, and resistance to power redistribution" (Arnstein, 1969: 217), among other things. In this way, they do reveal something intrinsic about hierarchy itself:

> what it means to treat another human being as somehow abstract ... and why something like that always seems to happen when some people claim to be inherently superior to others.
>
> (Graeber, 2007: 13)

Hierarchy thus makes visible and, at the same time, abstracts relations of superiority and inferiority. This structural view of criminal justice is descriptive, in one sense, but it doesn't provide insight into *how power works* within such hierarchies. It assumes the inevitability and immutability of these juridical relations, as if they just exist, naturally, without a history of how they came to be. It doesn't explain how these characteristics and assumptions shape and reinforce what we know about criminal justice, what is considered knowledge or "evidence", how that knowledge is produced, and who gets to produce it. To see beyond this simplified structure, to understand these dynamics and the various means by which power is exercised, requires other conceptual tools. Here a *post*structuralist perspective is useful.

Governmentality and technologies of power

Foucault[2] (1994: 570) tells us that "behind all knowledge, behind all knowing, what is at play is a struggle for power".[3] As we've suggested, the co-production of criminal justice knowledge is shaped by particular relations of power and involves specific kinds of negotiations and identity constructions that might be construed as this "struggle". The French word *lutte* (from the verb *lutter*, meaning to struggle or fight) is also the word for wrestling, which is perhaps a useful image to evoke the way co-production inevitably involves a degree of grappling or wrangling of power, whether overt or hidden, political or social, which gives the lie to a solely "juridical" or hierarchical form of power.

In Chapter 1, we identified characteristics or tendencies of contemporary criminal justice practice as having been shaped by the convergence of risk thinking, managerialism, and neoliberal notions of individualism, consumerism, personal responsibility, and "choice". These characteristics show how carceral logic extends beyond the criminal justice system through its interconnected web of psychological and rehabilitative interventions and techniques of control (Garland, 2001; Rose, 1998, 2000). Thinking with Foucault, we might invoke here the notion of *governmentality* to explain the diverse mechanisms through which power is exercised in the criminal justice field. From this perspective, rather than a fixed hierarchy that implies top-down, unilateral power of the sovereign state over its citizens, the rise of the modern bureaucratic state has seen relations of power multiplied and dispersed, and power "exercised today through a multitude of agencies and techniques, some of which are only loosely associated with the executives and bureaucracies of the formal organs of state" (Miller & Rose, 1998: 1). Thus, rather than "a negative, juridical idea of power", Foucault (1976/2012: 2) proposes "the idea of a technology of power".

Foucault's ideas help us understand how power works. The idea of *a technology of power* draws attention away from structures and hierarchies invested with power and towards the means and mechanisms – or technologies – through which power is exercised. He thus highlights the complexity and ambiguity of relations between institutions comprising what he called "the mesh of power" (1976/2012). For Foucault (1976/2012: 9), power is wielded through "political technologies", including "discipline", which he explained in this way:

> Discipline is basically the mechanism of power by which we come to exert control in the social body right down to the finest elements, by which we succeed in grabbing hold of the social atoms themselves, which is to say, individuals. Techniques for the individualization of power. How to monitor [*surveiller*] someone, how to control his conduct, his behavior, his aptitudes, how to intensify his performance, multiply his capacities, how to put him in a place where he will be most useful: this is what I mean by discipline.

Governmentality (think "governing"+"mentalities") involves governing the State, but also populations, organisations, individual bodies, and selves through multiple rationalities or ways of thinking about "how things are and how they ought to be" (Dean, 2010: 19). These rationalities extend beyond the discipline that Foucault describes above (what he also called the "conduct of conduct"), and into "a particular way of thinking about the kinds of problems that can and should be addressed by various authorities" (Miller & Rose, 1990: 2). The governmental "mesh of power" thus constitutes an "ensemble formed by the institutions, procedures, analyses and reflections, the calculations and tactics, that allow the exercise of this very specific albeit complex form of power" (Foucault, 1979: 20). In this way, it provides "an intellectual framework for rendering reality thinkable as a site of practical activity" (O'Malley, 1998: 156-7), which we now explore.

Key to this ensemble and its practical activities are two distinct yet intertwined elements: the programmatic and discursive aspects of governmentality (Miller & Rose, 1990). Miller and Rose (1990) identify its *programmatic* character in the "eternal optimism that a domain or a society could be administered better or more effectively, that reality is ... programmable" (p.4). Alongside this reformist zeal and the concrete ways it manifests (such as through programme evaluation and programmes of efficiency), governmentality is also *discursive*. In this respect, and similar to Foucault's technology of power, Miller and Rose (1990: 5) refer to "discourse" as "a technology of thought", which requires paying

> attention to the particular technical devices of writing, listing, numbering and computing that render a realm into discourse as a knowable, calculable and administrable object.

Here they are describing a way of ordering reality through processes that generate "facts" about a phenomenon that is thereby brought into existence as a thing that can be known. Just as "crime" itself is socially constructed, the world of crime control and criminal justice is rife with concepts brought into being through a combination of legal definition, popular culture, media usage, criminological adoption, and official classification (Rafter, 1990; Surette, 2015). Thus, as Miller and Rose (1990: 5) explain, governmental discourse involves ways of thinking *and* concrete practices of inscription:

> 'Knowing' an object in such a way that it can be governed is more than a purely speculative activity: it requires the invention of procedures of nota- tion, ways of collecting and presenting statistics, the transportation of these to centres where calculations and judgements can be made and so forth. It is through such procedures of inscription that the diverse domains of 'gov- ernmentality' are made up, that 'objects' such as the economy, the enter- prise, the social field and the family are rendered in a particular conceptual form and made amenable to intervention and regulation.

This concept of governmentality as a way of knowing – the idea of "know- ing" an object in such a way that it can be governed – offers a useful lens through which to consider the relationship between how language is used, how identity is defined, negotiated, and represented, and how the legitimacy of the criminal justice apparatus is established and maintained. It provides a way of understanding power and knowledge as complex, multiple phe- nomena that are always intertwined and always contested. It gives us a way to explore the promise of power-sharing that co-production holds out, on the one hand, and the risks of responsibilisation and neoliberal co-option (flagged in Chapter 1), on the other. This includes how the harnessing of "lived experience" may render experts-by-experience complicit in the gov- erning of others (Voronka, 2015).

Ideas of rationality

One of the main threads constituting Foucault's governmental mesh of power – within which reality is "programmable", and "knowability" is the means by which individuals and populations are regulated – is *rationality*. Yet, as David Graeber (2016) explains in *The Utopia of Rules*, within capitalist bureaucracies two "contradictory" and "strangely incoherent" (p.166) ideas of rationality prevail. One is "the application of logic, of pure thought untempered by emotions", implying neutrality and objectivity as the means and "the basis for scientific inquiry" (p.167). The other is an earlier conception of rationality as moral order, based on humans' ability to reason as the way to restrain our baser urges, and thus an end in itself. We can see these competing logics embedded in the machinery of criminal justice, where technocratic (governing by knowing "experts") and normative (what "should" be) goals converge, as the following illustrates.

Individuals subject to criminal justice intervention are translated into criminal justice "clients", that is, "consumers of the social services offered (mandated) through the criminal justice system" (Donohue & Moore, 2009: 320). This transactional relationship recasts criminalised people as "active participants in their own punishment and correction because they are choice making, free subjects" (Donohue & Moore, 2009: 320). On the one hand, each of us is responsibilised to minimise our own risk: "Each of us is to be our own rock" (Rose, 2000: 328). On the other hand, though, this dispersal of responsibility and "expertise" has implications for who is deemed the "rational subject" worthy of being included in this project, and who is to be excluded on the basis of "their lack of competence or capacity for responsible ethical self-management" (Rose, 2000: 333). In this way, "citizenship becomes conditional upon conduct" (p.335), implying a social hierarchy based on worthiness. The "rationality" of this moral order is irrational, in that people are judged not only by their past actions but also on what they might do in the future, which can only ever be known in retrospect.

Thinking about Foucault's mesh of power, in terms of how it might be experienced psycho-socially and spatially, brings to mind notions of "weight", "grip", or "tightness" (Crewe, 2011; Crewe & Ievins, 2021). The grip of the justice system and the power it has over people's lives has a rationality that is undone by the way it is experienced in human terms. As Crewe (2011: 522) describes, the term tightness conveys, viscerally,

> a sense of the way that power is experienced as both firm and soft, oppressive yet also somehow light. ... It conveys the way that power operates both closely and anonymously, working like an invisible

harness on the self. ... [I]t promotes the self-regulation of all aspects of conduct, addressing both the psyche and the body.

This tightness – "the close harness of penal power" (Crewe & Ievins, 2021: 60) – can bind people to the justice system and be felt in paradoxical ways: as a form of "envelopment" that may be "crushing and oppressive" (p.61), for instance; or the sense of being "seen" or "unseen" in ways that may be equally controlling (p.62). Thus, "technologies of power ... snag and entangle" people in a justice "web" (Crewe, 2011: 522).

So, to summarise our thinking in this chapter so far, power and hierarchy manifest in distinct and seemingly contradictory ways. On the one hand, we think about the criminal justice system in terms of hierarchy, which brings to mind a rigid top-down structure; hierarchy might certainly be *felt* experientially by those who feel power*less* in the system, as well as by those who wield power. On the other hand, we see power operating in dispersed, less visible, yet equally constraining ways. The language of "personal choice" alongside bureaucratic regulation, for instance, can leave people feeling on their own yet highly controlled – liberated, ordered, abandoned, and responsibilised by the state in unequal measure.

Thinking about power and hierarchy thus reveals layers of complexity that are important to consider when thinking about co-producing knowledge *about* criminal justice, *with* people involved with the criminal justice system. Thinking about power and hierarchy also highlights different ways of knowing, and implies that the view from below, the view from above, and the view from within might produce very different perspectives. If co-production means bringing these perspectives together, it also means bringing together different assumptions about and experiences of power, knowledge, and, indeed, reality. This raises a question about knowing: *how do we know what we know.*

Ways of knowing

Western knowledge systems tend to value certainty over doubt, objectivity over subjective experience, reason over intuition, and rationality over "irrationality". The us-and-them dichotomy that characterises criminal justice thinking can be traced to these dualistic assumptions, and mutually exclusive categories such as true/false, negative/positive, upon which Western logic rests. Since the 1970s, however, challenges to Eurocentric and androcentric ways of knowing have been gathering momentum and have taken many forms. Feminist thinkers, Indigenous standpoint epistemologists, anti-colonial, gender and disability scholars and activists, and poststructuralist writers and philosophers (including Foucault) have used critical theory and lived experience to highlight the limitations of Enlightenment thinking and its weddedness to objectivity, rationality, and logic as the basis of all knowledge. They have shown how different ways of knowing and being in the world exist, and persist, despite having been silenced and subjugated by dominant paradigms and the hierarchies that have sustained them. One such paradigm is the hierarchy of knowledge, or evidence, as mentioned in Chapter 1.

Hierarchies of knowledge, knowledge as hierarchy

As we have suggested, what is known about criminal justice is circumscribed by specific ways of knowing (epistemologies), ways of being (ontologies), and value systems (axiologies) that determine what is valorised as "knowledge" (or "evidence"), and what is *not* seen or valued. The holding up of "objectivity" as "scientific" (and therefore supreme) points to a particular Eurocentric epistemology, which as Mbembe (2015: 9) points out, "attributes truth only to the Western way of knowledge production [and] … disregards other epistemic traditions". In this way, as Tuck and Yang (2014: 245) assert: "Social science knowledge is settler-colonial knowledge [in that it] … refuses the agency, personhood, and theories of the researched … [and] limits the epistemologies of the colonized/colonizable/to-be-colonized". In drawing on anti-colonial thinking here, we are not suggesting that processes or experiences of criminalisation, per se, are equivalent to processes or experiences of colonisation. We recognise, though, that colonisers use/have used knowledge as a tool or strategy to subjugate other ways of knowing and being in the world. Knowledge can thus be understood as a site of domination and hegemony *and* a subjugating mechanism or process.

This second part of our analytical framework thus draws on the idea of hierarchies of knowledge (and knowledge as hierarchy) to examine how *knowing* and *knowledge* become means of dominating, appropriating, co-opting, and taking control over people, space, language, story, meaning, and identity in criminal justice. So, how does this idea fit with co-production? To explain how we are using this "knowledge hierarchy" lens, we identify two ways in which knowledge can be used to dominate, appropriate, and take control over people's lives: the power to define and the construction of identity; and the commodification of people's stories, especially of suffering and painful experience. Together these themes provide a useful frame of analysis for understanding the relations between co-producers in our case studies. We then consider what co-production might mean in terms of fundamentally shifting the ground of these relations in Australia's settler-colonial context and beyond.

The power to define, the construction of identity

As settler occupiers living and working on Aboriginal Country, we acknowledge the Traditional Owners of the land and honour the wisdom of First Nations Elders, past and present. Thinking about Western knowledge systems as having the power to define, we listen to Aboriginal scholar Irene Watson (2005: 47) when she writes that the settler-colonial "way of looking at us ... affected how we also looked at ourselves". We pay attention, too, to Māori filmmaker Merata Mita (1989, in Tuhiwai Smith, 2012: 117) explaining New Zealand's:

> history of people putting Maori under a microscope in the same way a scientist looks at an insect. The ones doing the looking are giving themselves the power to define.

Clearly, for colonised peoples, the power to define has explicit implications in terms of cultural genocide, which overlap with but are not limited to over-criminalisation and over-imprisonment. When we think about this power to define more broadly, and how it is carried and signified through language, it provides a useful lens through which to consider how criminalised people may come to view themselves and to be viewed by others, even long after their interaction with the legal system. In the language of criminalisation, stigmatising labels such as "criminal offender", "sex offender", "violent offender" – even "ex-offender" – can be "sticky" and hard to shift (Uggen & Blahnik, 2016; Denver *et al.* 2017). Similarly, the language of *risk* constructs certain people and groups as "risky" or "at risk" in ways that can become totalising (Hannah-Moffatt, 2005; Maurutto & Hannah-Moffatt, 2006). Who is *doing the looking* in these contexts? Who is holding *the power to define*?

Donohue and Moore (2009) suggest that correctional intervention turns people into justice "clients", as noted earlier, yet Nielsen and Kolind (2016) argue these institutional identities of "offender" and "client" are rarely distinct. Rather, identity construction is "fuzzy", oscillating between prison workers seeing prisoners as "real people" in one context, and "inmates" in another – or even "inmates-in-treatment" (p.145) – giving rise to blurred, varying, and context-dependent practices. This fuzziness underscores how the power to define, cloaked in the power to sanction, is embedded in every interaction between those subject to criminal justice intervention and those charged with its administration, and thus governs the lives of those imprisoned or court-ordered.

Just as knowledge can become a site of domination, and knowing a way of governing, the process of defining – identifying, naming, and categorising

– can be a way of imposing a hierarchy of truth, and thus foreclosing other ways of being and of knowing (Moreton-Robinson, 2004; Mbembe, 2015). First Nations' perspectives provide important insights into how dominant forms of knowledge narrate a past, demarcate the present, and foretell a future. Writing about the construction of Aboriginal identity through colonisation, for instance, Irene Watson (2005: 47) explains:

> The objective view is 'known' to be more reliable than our own oral stories about ourselves, which are too much 'inside the story', and not sufficiently distant from the subject. The state, in engaging the 'expert', imposes its way of knowing on us, and deploys colonial institutions to name us, and we are left to work with this, sifting the sand to find the kernel of our lives.

This "objective" view locks people out of their own stories, disregards people's capacity to narrate their own lives, and denies their expertise in their own experience. *Our own* stories are judged unreliable, our proximity to them is suspect. Thus, the power to define is also the power to construct people's identity – how they see themselves and how they are seen by others. This domination of identity is a form of epistemic violence and oppression (Spivak, 1988; Dotson, 2011). This is important when thinking about who holds power, who are the ones giving themselves power, and how power is shared in co-production relationships.

The commodification of pain

For many, collecting others' stories is the stock-in-trade of social science research (Spivak, 1988; Tuck & Yang, 2014). From this perspective, researchers, practitioners, and advocates can become "ventriloquis[ts] of the speaking subaltern" (Spivak, 2010: 27) when they assume authority over and authorship of the experiences of others. As bell hooks (1990: 343) writes:

> No need to hear your voice when I can talk about you better than you can speak about yourself.
> … I want to know your story. And then I will tell it back to you in a new way. … I am still author, authority. I am still coloniser the speaking subject and you are now at the center of my talk.

For those already excluded, marginalised, and frequently silenced, the sharing and retelling of private and painful experiences can be (re)traumatising. It is a form of cognitive injustice (de Sousa Santos, 2014). It constitutes, too, what Watson (2005: 41) describes as "biopiracy" – stealing and appropriating others' experiential knowledge, trading on people's stories of pain and adversity, and, in doing so, adding indignity.

The researcher profits from telling others' stories by assuming the role of professional narrator, clever interpreter of lived/living experiences of criminalisation, survival or redemption; benevolent conveyor of hard-to-reach tales of heroism, grit, or woe. Yet, in the commodification of criminal justice knowledge (Walters, 2003), somehow that larceny is sanitised, laundered, and rinsed away. We (researchers, advocates, and practitioners) don't recognise ourselves as pirates or purveyors of others' pain. We fail to acknowledge our command to "speak from that space in the margin that is a sign of deprivation, a wound, an unfulfilled longing. Only speak your pain" (hooks, 1990: 343). Walters (2003) attributes this to the emergence of "market-led criminology", highlighting the neoliberal context alluded to earlier. But we can refuse to work in this way. As researchers, advocates, and practitioners, we can resist "the draw to traffic theories that cast communities as in need of salvation" (Tuck & Yang, 2014: 245). We can eschew the commodification of others' stories, perhaps by allowing people to tell and thereby own their own stories. As Larissa Behrendt urges: "Use your voice when people need you to speak. And move out of the way, when [people] can speak for themselves".[4]

Co-production as disruptive?

Since the 1990s, calls to decolonise criminal justice and criminology have burgeoned (Deckert & Tauri, 2019). But what does this mean in the context of co-production and its potential for disrupting hierarchies of knowledge? It means changing the order of things, upending existing relations, and challenging dominant values. The rise of "convict criminology", in valorising "the authenticity of insider perspectives" (Richards & Ross, 2001: 178), is an example of this disruption. Arguably, though, the distinction between "ex-con" and "non-con" criminologists can reinforce the binary it seeks to challenge (Aresti & Darke, 2016). Co-production assumes the existence of multiple perspectives (different ways of seeing), and that understanding of any phenomenon is deepened by viewing it from different angles. Indeed, the "best" view is not always from the top. As Haraway (1988: 583) reminds us, "there is good reason to believe vision is better from below the brilliant space platforms of the powerful". Cunneen (2011: 254), for example, urges us "to consider how marginalized peoples may view criminal justice intervention as unjust", observing that:

> Western liberal democratic states define their criminal justice systems as neutral, fair and universal in their application, indeed their legitimacy

demands that these principles be upheld. Yet it is clear that many Indigenous peoples see state criminal justice systems as oppressive.

Similarly, Cunneen (2011: 258) points to the need to emphasise "the perspective of the marginalized in both understanding and in responding to 'over-representation' in the criminal justice system". We consider the potential of co-production to introduce different perspectives and to thus allow disruptive forms of plurality, multiple ways of knowing. In this way, criminal justice knowledge, whilst hierarchical in the ways we've described earlier, can also disrupt and expand what is known (and how it is known) about the structures, inequities, impacts, and experiences of criminalising processes. Writing about policing and counter-policing of Aboriginal communities in Australia, for example, Amanda Porter (2016) highlights "the importance of grounding analyses with reference to localized Indigenous justice practices" (p.560). Porter suggests this involves centring local Indigenous voices and perspectives, working with local Indigenous governance, and incorporating Indigenous methodologies. The Koorie Youth Council's (KYC 2018) *Ngaga-dji* report ("Hear me" in Woi Wurrung), featuring the voices and perspectives of criminalised Aboriginal young people in Victoria, Australia, is an example of the kind of knowledge that disrupts and expands in these ways.

In this book, therefore, we challenge the idea of "knowledge" as hierarchical, fixed, and rooted in specific power relations that infer or confer expertise. Seeing this idea of knowledge as inherently dominating, we seek to explore how/whether co-production can uncover other ways of knowing, other ways of seeing (different ontologies, epistemologies, and axiologies), and how this makes room for *multiple knowledges*. Of course, we acknowledge risks and limitations, too. Critically, while co-production promises a new approach to thinking, doing and making criminal justice, it also threatens to shore up the structures and relations that embody and perpetuate historic injustices and inequalities, evident in the ongoing over-criminalisation and over-imprisonment of Indigenous people (Anthony, 2016). We concede that intentions alone are never enough to disrupt entrenched structures and traditions (Snelgrove *et al.* 2014). Co-production in and of itself, as either discourse or practice, cannot necessarily achieve structural change or genuine shifts in power. As a buzzword, it risks succumbing to a "fetishisation of method" (Gordon, 2014). As Haraway (1988: 583) warns, there is a danger "of romanticizing and/or appropriating the vision of the less powerful while claiming to see from their positions".

The trick may lie in constantly reflecting on the power dynamics at play – being reflexive – and in learning and practising "how to see from below" (Haraway, 1988: 584). "Vision is always a question of the power to see", Haraway (1988: 585) tells us, "and perhaps of the violence implicit in our visualizing practices". We might add that knowing is a question of the power to speak – and the power to define – and perhaps of the violence implicit in our knowledge production practices, for example, the epistemic violence of locking people out of their own stories, or denying people's expertise in their own experience (Dotson, 2011). It is important, therefore, to consider how traditional hierarchies of knowledge about crime and criminal justice have been generated and sustained. We need to examine the role of academic and practical criminology and social work in that endeavour, to ask *whose knowledge* has been smothered and suppressed in the process? And, in challenging and subverting this process, we invite an attitudinal shift towards humility, reflexivity, and openness, to recognise *as interlocutors* (Istratii *et al.* 2018) those we condemn, exclude, manage, and other. To sit at the table together.

In Part II, we present case studies illustrating different aspects of co-production in four criminal justice-related contexts:

- Chapter 3 is set in a prison context, with formerly imprisoned men;
- Chapter 4 looks at projects involving criminalised women;
- Chapter 5 explores practitioner perspectives on co-production; and
- Chapter 6 considers co-production with First Nations communities.

To construct these case studies, we sought and received institutional ethics approval.[5] We used a semi-structured interview schedule to gather qualitative insights from experts involved in co-production about the what, who, why, and how of their projects. Each case study is presented as a whole "story", written by one or more of the authors, with the final version approved by the co-producers. Stories or narratives are ways that we make sense of the world and tell each other about our world (Bruner, 1991, in Thomas, 2021: 131); they allow for a holistic, contextualised representation, rather than being told through disaggregated quotes. Methodologically, case studies are an appropriate approach given the paucity of knowledge on co-production in criminal justice (Yin, 2009; Thomas, 2021). We selected cases based on our networks and knowledge of who was engaging in innovative practices in this area. We are aware that gaining a full picture of any phenomenon, event, or project requires seeing it from a range of vantage points and hearing a diversity of voices and perspectives. In this respect, all of our case studies have limitations. Our main aim was to maximise the scope of examples, the range of sites, and the roles of the interviewees; our aim was not to say the last word about co-production in criminal justice but to begin the conversation. The seven case studies, presented over the next four chapters, provide that starting point.

As purposefully selected examples, these cases are not meant to be representative. Drawing on a small number of cases allows for deep exploration of the complexity of factors and processes at play and gives a rich and detailed description of each story and its context. Case studies also allow the reader to make their own interpretations. Our case studies are focused predominantly on co-production with people who have experienced criminalisation, yet we might equally have considered workers in the system, victims and other community members affected by crime as co-producers[6] (as alluded to in the practitioners' case studies and Keeping on Country). The case studies are also weighted towards a focus on prison and post-imprisonment. This is partly because these examples fell within our purview. It is also because we think of the criminal justice system as a complex network of interrelated practices and processes that centre on punishment and "correction", and these can be seen to radiate from the prison, its beating heart. In these respects, while our case studies offer a small range of criminal justice contexts, they represent a sample of critical cases (Yin, 2009) that allow a view of co-production "from *several* directions" (Thomas, 2021: 5) and have lessons for all of us working to co-produce knowledge in some form of criminal justice setting.

Each chapter, each case study, is different. We did not aim for uniformity. Chapters 4 and 5 present multiple case studies, whereas Chapters 3 and 6 present a single case study each. These examples thus provide more context and finer-grained detail, which aids our growing understanding of what it means to co-produce criminal justice knowledge in Australia. We had other reasons for giving space to these two case studies. We included User Voice as a long-standing example of co-production that has been operating in England since 2009, but also as an organisation in the process of being established in Australia. Chapter 6's case study – Keeping on Country – focuses on two Indigenous communities in Far North Queensland. Given the long-standing and disproportionately high rates of criminalisation and imprisonment of Aboriginal and Torres Strait Islander peoples in Australia and the more recent and increasing awareness that responses and research need to be led and shaped by First Nations communities, we needed to devote space to this example.

Our case studies differ in voice and style too. Chapter 3 focuses on prison councils run by User Voice, a UK-based not-for-profit organisation led by self-described "ex-offenders". This case study was prepared by Diana, a Melbourne-based criminologist, whose research on men's experience of release from prison brought her into contact with User Voice in Australia and England. It is based on informal conversations and fieldnotes gathered over two years.

Chapter 4 presents three case studies: a 12-episode podcast project (Birds Eye View); a community support service established by and for women with lived prison experience (Seeds of Affinity), both in Australia; and a research project based in Ireland[7] (The Mothers' Project). Catherine, a Melbourne-based social work academic, who has researched issues of women and imprisonment over some 15 years, including her doctoral research, wrote this chapter based on her interviews with one woman in each project.

Chapter 5 presents two case studies from practitioners' perspectives: a peer-mentoring programme in a men's prison (Straight Talking), and a study with young men in youth detention (Youth Justice). Based on their interviews with the practitioners, this chapter was written by Catherine and Shelley, Melbourne-based social workers with direct practice and research experience, and a specific interest in collaborative practices, in and around youth and adult criminal justice in various jurisdictions.

Chapter 6 explores the Keeping on Country research project in Far North Queensland. This case study was prepared by Maggie, a Sydney-based non-Indigenous law/social work academic and criminologist, who – after hearing about the project and reading published work arising from it – interviewed two of the researchers via Zoom: the lead academic, based at James Cook University in Townsville, and the psychologist working at the two communities' healing and well-being centres. As we note in Chapter 6, Maggie was not able to travel to interview the two other researchers or any of the community partners. We acknowledge this is a limitation.

We recognise that history, politics, and social structure are embedded in policy and discourse that surrounds the doing of research, and shape how knowledge is both produced and privileged. While we seek to examine the complexities of co-production, acknowledging our settler-colonial standpoint and the need to critically reflect on and address how colonisation has shaped and continues to shape social, political, and legal structures and relations in contemporary Australia, our approach has led us to ask questions of ourselves. By interviewing only the white, non-Aboriginal co-producers, are we reproducing the power relations that have dominated since colonisation? Are we participating in some of the practices that we seek to challenge, in terms of reifying power, defining parameters, silencing voices?

Notes

1 In later chapters we use "Justice" (capitalised) as shorthand for all the ways in which 'criminal justice' and the 'criminal justice system' works and manifests. In this chapter, we refer to 'criminal justice' to lay the conceptual foundations for the emergence of Justice as the character of and a character in the story of Co-production & Criminal Justice we tell in this book (see Chapter 7, footnote 46).

2 Foucault was the critical theorist who, with his book *Discipline and Punish* (published in English in 1977), brought poststructuralist theory to criminology and criminal justice (Rafter, 1990: 380).

3 This is our translation of Foucault's (1994: 570) words, "derrière tout savoir, derrière toute connaissance, ce qui est en jeu, c'est une lutte de pouvoir".

4 At the 2021 Rebellious Lawyering (RebLaw) Australia Conference, as tweeted by @melissayvonne7 (Twitter, Sept 24, 2021) and retweeted by @LarissaBehrendt.

5 Monash University Human Research Ethics Committee (MUHREC) Project ID: 21471.

6 We acknowledge the frequent overlap between "victims" and "offenders".

7 A few words here about why we included an Irish case study in a book focused on Australia: Catherine met Sinead via Twitter some years ago, shared her concern about the impact of maternal imprisonment, and knew of the work she was doing. Although the contexts are different, there are many similarities in the experiences of imprisoned mothers in both countries, not least being a minority group in the overall prison system and the implications of this. Having lived and worked as a social worker in statutory systems in the North of Ireland herself, Catherine saw many parallels, and we felt the lessons from this research example would be meaningful and transferable.

References

Anthony, T (2016) Deaths in custody: 25 years after the royal commission, we've gone backwards, *The Conversation*, April 13.

Aresti, A & Darke, S (2016) Practicing convict criminology: Lessons learned from British academic activism, *Critical Criminology*, 24(4): 533–547.

Arnstein, S (1969) A ladder of citizen participation, *Journal of the American Institute of Planners*, 35(4): 216–224.

Bruner, J (1991) The narrative construction of reality, *Critical Inquiry*, 18(1): 1–21.

Crewe, B (2011) Depth, weight, tightness: Revisiting the pains of imprisonment, *Punishment & Society*, 13(5): 509–529.

Crewe, B & Ievins, A (2021) 'Tightness', recognition and penal power, *Punishment & Society*, 23(1): 47–68.

Cunneen, C (2011) Postcolonial perspectives for criminology. In M Bosworth & C Hoyle (Eds.), *What is criminology?* Oxford: OUP, pp. 249–266.

Dean, M (2010) *Governmentality: Power and rule in modern society*, 2nd edn. London: Sage.

Deckert, A & Tauri, J (2019) Editorial, *Decolonization of Criminology & Justice*, 1(1): 1–4.

Denver, M, Pickett, J & Bushway, S (2017) The language of stigmatization and the mark of violence: Experimental evidence on the social construction and use of criminal record stigma, *Criminology*, 55(3): 664–690.

De Sousa Santos, B (2014) *Epistemologies of the south: Justice against epistemicide*. Oxon/New York: Routledge.

Donohue, E & Moore, D (2009) When is an offender not an offender?: Power, the client and shifting penal subjectivities, *Punishment & Society*, 11(3): 319–336.

Dotson, K (2011) Tracking epistemic violence, tracking practices of silencing, *Hypatia*, 26(2): 236–257.

Foucault, M (1976 [2012]) The mesh of power (trans. C Chitty), *Viewpoint Magazine*, September 12, 2012.

Foucault, M (1977) *Discipline and punish: The birth of the prison*. New York: Pantheon Books.

Foucault, M (1979) Governmentality, *Ideology and Consciousness*, 6: 5–21.

Foucault, M (1994) La vérité et les formes juridiques, *Dits et Ecrits 1954–1988*, Vol. II: 1970-1975, No.139, Gallimard, Paris, pp. 538–646.

Garland, D (1996) The limits of the sovereign state: Strategies of crime control in contemporary society, *British Journal of Criminology*, 36(4): 445–471.

Garland, D (2001) *The culture of control*. Oxford: Oxford University Press.

Graeber, D (2007) *Possibilities: Essays on hierarchy, rebellion, and desire*. Edinburgh: AK Press.

Graeber, D (2016) *The Utopia of rules: On technology, stupidity, and the secret joys of bureaucracy*. Brooklyn/London: Melville House.

Gordon, LR (2014) Disciplinary decadence and the decolonisation of knowledge, *Africa Development*, 39(1): 81–92.

Hannah-Moffatt, K (2005) Criminogenic needs and the transformative risk subject: Hybridizations of risk/need in penality, *Punishment & Society*, 7(1): 29–51.

Haraway, D (1988) Situated knowledges: The science question in feminism and the privilege of partial perspective, *Feminist Studies*, 14(3): 575–599.

hooks, b (1990) Postmodern blackness. In *Yearning: Race, gender, and cultural politics*, 2nd ed. Boston, MA: South End Press, pp. 23–31.

Istratii, R, Hirmer, M & Lim, I (2018) Decolonisation in praxis, editorial I, *SOAS Journal of Postgraduate Research*, 11: 6–9.

KYC (2018) *Ngaga-dji report*. Melbourne: Koorie Youth Council. https://www.ngaga-djiproject.org.au/

Maurutto, P & Hannah-Moffat, K (2006) Assembling risk and the restructuring of penal control, *British Journal of Criminology*, 46(3): 438–454.

Mbembe, A (2015) *Decolonizing knowledge and the question of the archive*. Johannesburg: Wits Institute for Social and Economic Research, University of the Witwatersrand.

Miller, P & Rose, N (1990) Governing economic life, *Economy & Society*, 19(1): 1–31.

Mita, M (1989) Merata Mita on..., *The New Zealand Listener*, 14 October, p. 30.

Moreton-Robinson, A (2004) *Whitening race: Essays in social and cultural criticism*. Canberra: Aboriginal Studies Press.

Nielsen, B & Kolind, T (2016) Offender and/or client? Fuzzy institutional identities in prison-based drug treatment in Denmark, *Punishment & Society*, 18(2): 131–150.

O'Malley, P (1998) Indigenous governance. In M Dean & B Hindess (Eds.), *Governing Australia: Studies in contemporary rationalities of government*. Cambridge: Cambridge University Press, pp. 156–172.

Porter, A (2016) Decolonizing policing: Indigenous patrols, counter-policing and safety, *Theoretical Criminology*, 20(4): 548–565.

Rafter, NH (1990) The social construction of crime and crime control, *Journal of Research in Crime & Delinquency*, 27(4): 376–389.

Richards, SC & Ross, JI (2001) Introducing the new school of convict criminology, *Social Justice*, 28(1): 177–190.

Rose, N (1998) Governing risky individuals: The role of psychiatry in new regimes of control, *Psychiatry, Psychology & Law*, 5(2): 177–195.

Rose, N (2000) Government and control, *British Journal of Criminology*, 40(2): 321–339.

Slay, J & Stephens, L (2013) *Co-production in mental health: A literature review*. London: New Economics Foundation.

Snelgrove, C, Dhamoon, R & Corntassel, J (2014) Unsettling settler colonialism: The discourse and politics of settlers, and solidarity with Indigenous nations, *Decolonization: Indigeneity, Education & Society*, 3(2): 1–32.

Spivak, GC (1988) Can the subaltern speak? In C Nelson & L Grossberg (Eds.), *Marxism and the interpretation of culture*. Basingstoke: Macmillan Education, pp. 271–313.

Spivak, GC (2010) Can the subaltern speak? In R Morris (Ed.), *Can the subaltern speak? Reflections on the history of an idea*. New York: Columbia University Press, pp. 21–80.

Surette, R (2015) Thought bite: A case study of the social construction of a crime and justice concept, *Crime, Media, Culture*, 11(2): 105–135.

Thomas, G (2021) *How to do your case study*, 3rd edn. London: Sage.

Tuck, E & Yang, WE (2014) R-words: Refusing research. In D Paris & M T Winn (Eds.), *Humanizing research: Decolonizing qualitative inquiry with youth and communities*. Thousand Oaks, CA: Sage Publications, pp. 223–247.

Tuhiwai Smith, L (2012) *Decolonizing methodologies: Research and Indigenous peoples*, 2nd edn. London/New York: Zed Books.

Uggen, C & Blahnik, L (2016) The increasing stickiness of public labels. In J Shapland, S Farrall & A Bottoms (Eds.), *Global perspectives on desistance*. Oxon/New York: Routledge, pp. 222–243.

Voronka, J (2015) *Troubling inclusion: The politics of peer work and 'people with lived experience' in mental health interventions*. PhD thesis, University of Toronto, Canada.

Walters, R (2003) New modes of governance and the commodification of criminological knowledge, *Social & Legal Studies*, 12(1): 5–26.

Watson, I (2005) Settled and unsettled spaces: Are we free to roam? *Australian Critical Race & Whiteness Studies Association Journal*, 1: 41–52.

Yin, RK (2009) *Case study research: Design and methods*, 4th edn. London: Sage.

Part 2

3 User Voice prison councils

This is a case study of the co-production of knowledge about prison and imprisonment – from what it means to live and work in prison and to have a voice in its day-to-day running, to the role of ex-prisoners as peer mentors, leaders, and educators. It is focused on User Voice, a UK-based organisation (with an emerging Australian presence) that works with and across different forms and levels of co-production, including service design and delivery, practice improvement, policy development, and governance. In this respect, it uniquely illustrates a wide range of practices and processes that all come under the co-production umbrella. This case study is informed by Diana Johns' conversations with Mark Johnson and other User Voice staff in Australia and England, including when Diana visited User Voice sites in Birmingham and London in 2018 and 2019.

People's lives intersect with the prison in different ways. Some of us have little to do with prisons at all; others' lives intersect with the prison on an everyday basis, either as a workplace or as a place of legal confinement. Yet all of us "know" *something* about prison, even if our notions are shaped solely by stereotypes and popular images from films or television. To some extent, we are all "penal spectators" (Brown, 2009), in that we participate in the reproduction of shared cultural imagery, tropes, and narratives about prison and prisoners, regardless of whether we have set foot inside a correctional institution. This spectatorship can blind us to the realities and complexities of the prison as a social and political institution, what it *does* and what it *can* do in terms of achieving the aims of rehabilitation, for instance, or its capacity to keep us safe from the harms of crime and violence. It can preclude our deeper understanding of what it means to live and work in a prison. How it can be hardening, stultifying, and dehumanising. How it can warp and undermine "normal" human relationships by normalising violence and retribution. How it isolates and alienates people from each other.

DOI: 10.4324/9780429328657-5

The "us-and-them" culture that breeds inside prison is mirrored in the suspicion and distrust with which ex-prisoners are viewed outside. User Voice is
a UK-based "user-led" organisation dedicated to breaking down this separation through facilitating collaboration and dialogue between criminal justice
service users and service providers. Guided by the principle that *only offenders can stop re-offending*, the prison council model it has developed provides
a structure for democratic participation and collaborative problem-solving,
offering "a chance for everyone on the wing or on licence to have their say
with ideas and solutions"[1] User Voice thus aims to give people with convic-
tions a voice and ensure that this voice is heard by decision-makers, to build "a
culture of continuous improvement within criminal justice"[2] – institutionally
and individually – and to create opportunities for rehabilitation and recovery.

Employees and volunteers work with empathy based on their own lived
experience: "We know what it's like to be locked up in prison. To have drug,
alcohol, and mental health issues. To live on the streets". This shared experience grounds *authenticity* as one of User Voice's core values[3] – "We bring
our experiences to the table. We are the evidence base" – which eschews
tokenism and demands recognition and representation:

> #LivedExperience isn't tokenistic at User Voice. 85% of us have been
> in prison or on probation and 42% started as council members while
> still serving their sentence
>
> (@uservoiceorg, Twitter, Dec 16, 2020)

*****

8.30, a wet Tuesday morning in North London, late September 2019.[4]
I've arrived at Her Majesty's Prison (HMP) Pentonville, where I've
arranged to meet Garry from User Voice. It's pouring outside and I
squeeze into the damp entrance area, umbrella dripping, wondering
how I'm going to know who Garry is. … I reach the window to hand
over my passport, say my name, and I hear a voice behind me – is that
Diana?

After a short delay – my name's not on the list – Garry always has
trouble here, more than at any other prison, but a phone call sorts it –
I'm given a lanyard and we're ready to go in. Garry leads me to the key
room. Remarkably, given he was a prisoner himself, he seems to have
access to the whole prison. This speaks to the uniqueness of User Voice
– most of its staff are "ex-offenders" – and the esteem this organisation
and its workers have garnered across the UK's penal estate.

Garry leads me through gates and doorways, corridors and wings, a
nineteenth-century rabbit warren with bars and walls painted white to

conceal the smells and grime and despair simmering below the paint-work, gloss applied in anticipation of a recent visit from the HMIP Inspectors. It didn't fool them, Garry tells me, they still saw the cock-roaches running everywhere. The prison is on lockdown this morning due to scheduled staff training, which throws Garry's plans to show me around the wings, but it's okay because some of the council members will be unlocked.

We make our way to the resettlement room, a large sparsely furnished space with a few posters on the walls, below high windows framing the grey sky. We sit and talk about User Voice and its work, and how it takes a truly collaborative approach – albeit a slightly chaotic one behind the scenes – which is organised and systematic in the way it promotes and facilitates democratic process and engagement. Garry tells me a high-level staff member, newly appointed, said they had never seen an organisation so chaotic yet so effective. The prison councils are generally voted in every year in an election in each prison, but here – because of a new Governor – there have been some teething problems and the election planned for June has not yet gone ahead. Nevertheless, the prison has paid User Voice for a twelve-month contract to set up and run the council, indicating clear intention and commitment to the process.

Soon the council members arrive – only six today rather than the usual twenty or so – along with one of the governors and the diversity worker to talk about Black History Month (I suspect this may be an example of what Garry had mentioned as the process whereby the prison tries to use the council for its own purposes). But today, because of the small group and interest in the topic, Gary allows this discussion to take over the meeting. It means I don't have a chance to be properly introduced and my presence as an observer explained, but I meet and shake hands with each of the men individually, so I feel welcome enough. They are a mixed bunch, from early twenties to mid-forties, with different experiences of this place and other prisons.

The prison in many ways would prefer the council members to be the best-behaved, most compliant prisoners, but that goes against the philosophy of challenging power structures to bring about real criminal justice change, which is what Garry says User Voice is doing. It's about engaging as many people as possible, regardless of their histories. The secret, he says, is not just the model and the flexibility for people to implement it in their own way, but in the relationships and understanding that people build and bring to the work, and the genuine commitment to making things better.

For Garry, it's not just 'work', it's living and breathing it. Like User Voice founder, Mark Johnson, Garry's childhood was marred by alcohol, drugs, and violence; he spent years in secure care, secure welfare, youth detention, and later, adult prison. 'I'm an ex-offender', he reminds me, 'my hypervigilance is high'; this work, however, transforms that lived experience into an 'edge'. For this work, it's an occupational requirement.

*****

Mark Johnson's experience of physical and emotional violence, and deprivation and abuse – depicted in his book *Wasted* (2007) – led to years of drug-fuelled self-destruction and criminal justice entanglement, through gradual recovery and "getting clean" at 29, to becoming a self-described rehabilitated offender. Street-smart, entrepreneurial, and keen to help others as others had helped him; he first set up a tree-lopping business to employ people with criminal records and then founded User Voice in 2009, receiving charity status in 2010.

For Johnson, the prison is part of a broader system of social policies and practices that should support and assist people to change their lives and their communities for the better, but that fails because the people most directly affected are too often excluded from decision-making. People need incentives to change, he argues, and – rather than responses that emphasise punishment and control – there is a more urgent need to recognise "the power of the community to change itself" and "the emotional deprivation at the heart of the problem" of crime and violence (Johnson 2009a). He insists that "only by consulting fully with marginalised people about what policies are working, and what their real needs are, can we build a successful system" (Johnson, 2009b). Full consultation means listening to and valuing people's experience *as expertise*, which requires another element of the User Voice approach: helping people learn to present their experiences "in a way that makes them understandable and usable by policy-makers" (Johnson, 2008).

User Voice was founded on the belief that listening to "users of the criminal justice system" – prisoners and ex-prisoners – can make the system "more humane, productive, and rehabilitation-based" (Johnson 2008). User Voice's flagship initiative is its Prison and Community Council model, designed and delivered in prisons to help "prisoners, staff and governors co-produce interventions that aid rehabilitation and improve the living conditions" (Johnson, 2012), and to improve services for people serving orders in the community. In 2009 and 2011, User Voice established the first of their prison councils in two UK prisons. In 2021, 30 councils, comprising over 600 participants, operate in prisons and the community[5] across the United Kingdom.

In-depth studies of prison councils in England (Solomon & Edgar, 2004; Schmidt, 2013; Barry *et al.* 2016; Schmidt, 2020 – the latter three focused on User Voice specifically) have shown that, overwhelmingly, prison councils are seen as beneficial for and by prisons and prisoners. The benefits include "the value of dialogue" (Solomon & Edgar, 2004: 22) and communication, to alleviate and moderate tensions and conflicts, and to explain decision-making to prisoners, which can improve prison life generally. Schmidt studied User Voice councils in three prisons and found that principles implicit in democratic participation – "responsibility, voice and choice, generativity, recognition, contributing to a civic community, [and] a collective effort towards betterment" – were valued by everyone involved in council activities (2012 in Schmidt, 2020: 23).

While prison councils are neither new nor unique to User Voice, four distinct aspects differentiate the User Voice model from other approaches to prisoner representation or advocacy (Schmidt, 2013):

1. User Voice is an independent organisation contracted by individual prisons to run the councils;
2. User Voice is led and run by ex-offenders who model roles and behaviour for other prisoners;
3. The User Voice council model is based on principles of democratic participation and "values of equal representation and giving prisoners a voice" (p.12); and
4. User Voice retains flexibility to adapt to and meet the needs of each unique prison setting.

Generally, this approach entails teaching, modelling, and supporting the process of democratic participation. In the development of a prison council, User Voice staff support prisoners to form parties around specific issues and hold annual elections – where prisoners vote for a party based on their policy platform. An official town crier announces the results throughout the prison – priorities are determined by the elected party gathering constituents' views and suggestions across the prison, which are then presented to the prison governor to be acted upon. The issues and priorities vary across prisons, but the process of identifying problems and exploring possible solutions is common across councils, as this prisoner participant describes:

> *That's the first thing – we've identified a problem and then we look at the options. It's like a puzzle where you keep moving the pieces around to see what fits. ... If the problem is violence on canteen day, for example, we'd map out possible solutions: Could packs be delivered door to door? By staff or prisoners? What about confidentiality? And so on, until we find something that works. ... Everyone comes with their own knowledge and experience, so that informs the whole process.*
>
> (CP in Schmidt, 2020: 99)

This problem-solving process is collaborative in a way few processes in prison are:

> *Just about everything in prison is about the negatives or the deficits ... we're [prisoners] turned into robots that get told what to do and when to do it. ... But when we get the chance to do the opposite it really changes your whole way of thinking. ... Instead of just saying everything is shite and listing all the problems, let's flip that and look at the solutions.*
>
> (CP in Schmidt, 2020: 99)

User Voice has demonstrated considerable success through their councils: in 2017–2018, for example, council members put forward 210 proposals for change to prison governors and probation chief executives, of which 94% were accepted and implemented.[6] During the COVID-19 pandemic, when prisoners experienced increased isolation and lockdown, User Voice councils directly engaged nearly 23,000 people in prison and in the community in 2020 (compared to 44,000 in 2019), despite the restrictions, using a range of digital means to gather people's concerns about social isolation and mental health.[7] For instance, feedback from women at one prison included: "now I'm not able to associate with others so I'm completely isolated" and "All this time spent in my room is severely affecting my mental health", to which the suggested solution proposed by the prison council included: "Unlock all residents every morning to allow them to freely access communal areas and engage with other residents whilst still social distancing" (@uservoiceorg, Twitter, Dec 3, 2020).

In terms of political engagement, a User Voice survey of voting intentions showed striking increases among prisoners across three prisons. While only 35% had previously voted in General Elections, this jumped to 79% of prisoners involved in the prison councils, indicating their intention to vote in future.

> *These striking findings show that Prison Council elections awaken prisoners' interest in the national democratic process. These results are particularly encouraging because ex-prisoners who fulfil their civic responsibilities by voting are more likely to show responsibility in other areas of their lives, demonstrating more active citizens.*[8]

These findings illustrate the pedagogical ramifications of User Voice prison councils in terms of active participation and citizenship. Schmidt (2020: 98) conceives "active citizenship" as "a status affirmed or denied through everyday relational encounters with others in a collective pursuit of a shared purpose" and considers the extent to which democracy can be learnt via the council as a "school of citizenship", exploring "the role of power within and around the council" (p.98). The prisoner quoted earlier gives insight into how power shifts within and through the council structure, first describing the de-responsibilising effects of penal institutionalisation:

> *Just about everything in prison is about the negatives or the deficits – it prevents this, it takes away this, it limits this, we're [prisoners] turned into robots that get told what to do and when to do it and how to do it.*

This is contrasted against the prison council as an opportunity "to do the opposite", to contribute and collaborate in constructive dialogue, which has powerful transformative potential:

> *it really changes your whole way of thinking. It's like it opens up a world you didn't know was there. ... And you know, people get excited about solutions because that opens things up too, you know, like look at all these prospects we've got now. It's energising.*
>
> (in Schmidt, 2020: 99)

In exploring the workings of User Voice councils in three English prisons, Schmidt (2013) identified consistent themes suggesting the benefits of participating in councils for prisoners and prison staff, including the impact on prisoner identities. Being "treated like a person" and seen as a "council member" rather than a "prisoner" or "offender" helped prisoners develop confidence, skills, and self-worth, which shaped prisoners' view of themselves and their future. Engaging in constructive dialogue with a focus on improvement generated "a sense of collective responsibility" that permeated the wider prison culture (p.13). The collaborative work of the councils has helped reconfigure prisoner–staff relations based on "increased levels of recognition and trust" (p.13). Further, in terms of tempering the prevailing milieu of tension, fear, and volatility, the council helped prisoners to "feel more secure and certain" (p.13), which has clear implications for the security and well-being of everyone living and working in the prison and, in the longer term, in the wider community. The importance of ex-prisoners running the councils was noted by prisoners and staff, as these quotes indicate (Schmidt, 2013: 14):

> *we feel like we can relate to them. ... They've done their own bird, yeah, so they can tell us their first-hand experience. ... It shows that if you're an ex-offender you can do something different; something positive.*
>
> [Prisoner]

> *The one thing that ex-lads [ex-offenders] add to any jail is that they add a lot of stability; a lot of influence ... because ... a lot of these lads here don't know ... what to expect, and we're not very good at telling them, because actually, we don't know, half the time.*
>
> [Staff member]

As well as these benefits, however, Schmidt identified barriers to the councils' successful implementation. She notes "undercurrents of resentment, punitive values, and a belief that prisoners did not deserve to have a voice" (2013: 16) among some staff in the early stages of council development, as this quote exemplifies:

> *You know, they're in here for a reason. They shouldn't be rewarded for that. They can't just start requesting whatever they want ... that's not how prison works.*

Staff in other prisons, however, welcomed the council, as this senior staff member reflected:

> *[It] directs offenders to act, vote, discuss matters reasonably. ... It also gave offenders direction, a purpose, responsibility, and staff saw the positive influence and welcomed it from then on.*

Thus, despite some initial misgivings and fears about "giving prisoners too much power" (Schmidt, 2013: 16), as one User Voice employee observed, by "breaking down those barriers between the con and staff, and making cons and staff work together a little bit better" (p.16), councils generally improve staff–prisoner relationships. According to Schmidt (2013: 17), four key elements determine a council's success: (1) the prison governor's commitment and dedication to the project; (2) the staff's acceptance of and engagement with the council at every stage of its development; (3) the council bringing about positive change and making it clear how that was achieved, thereby maintaining its "legitimacy and effectiveness"; and (4) User Voice providing adequate and ongoing support for its staff and council at each site, thereby demonstrating professionalism and reliability.

The challenge for User Voice, in seeking "to improve rehabilitation through collaboration" (User Voice, 2015: 1) by centring the voices of lived experience, rests on power structures (government and prison authorities) having "to cede ... some power and responsibility" (Johnson, 2009a). Yet, in terms of empowering people to participate, "too often the chaotic and vulnerable are set up to fail" (Johnson, 2010). For User Voice, failure is part of the story, an opportunity to learn; to "bounce back and keep on going … [and to] support each other in the face of adversity".[9] "Democracy and imprisonment" may indeed "make for strange bedfellows" (Schmidt, 2020: 25), yet User Voice's commitment to "ordering chaos"[10] suggests they do not shy away from such challenges. It appears, to an outsider at least, that fearlessness, solidarity, optimism, and resilience drive this co-production democracy machine.

Notes

1 https://www.User Voice.org/home/what-we-do
2 https://www.User Voice.org/home/what-we-do
3 https://www.User Voice.org/home/who-we-are/
4 This section is based on reflections recorded by Diana Johns following a visit to the User Voice Prison Council at HMP Pentonville.
5 Including Youth Offending Teams (YOTs), Community Rehabilitation Companies (CRCs), and the National Probation Service (NPS) (see https://www.User Voice.org/home/what-we-do).
6 Email communication with User Voice, Australia, 2019.
7 Email communication with User Voice, Australia, 2019.
8 Email communication with User Voice, Australia, 2019.
9 'Our Values', https://www.uservoice.org/home/who-we-are/.
10 'Our Values', https://www.uservoice.org/home/who-we-are/.

References

Barry, M, Weaver, B, Liddle, M & Schmidt, B (2016) *Evaluation of the user voice prison and community councils: Final report*. London: User Voice.

Brown, M (2009) *The culture of punishment: Prison, society, and spectacle*. New York: NYU Press.

Johnson, M (2007) *Wasted: A childhood stolen, an innocence betrayed, a life redeemed*. London: Little Brown.

Johnson, M (2008) Ex-criminals have a lot to say, now government must listen, *The Guardian*. September 17.

Johnson, M (2009a) Academics can't see through the 'feral youth' smokescreen, *The Guardian*. February 18.

Johnson, M (2009b) Teenagers need the power to step off the trouble train, *The Guardian*. April 15.

Johnson, M (2010) Get ex-offenders on board with Clarke's radical prison plans, *The Guardian*. December 15.

Johnson, M (2012) User Voice Promo, YouTube, Oct 12. https://youtu.be/qCaJGzyRBEc

Schmidt, B (2013) User voice and the prison council model: A summary of key findings from an ethnographic exploration of participatory governance in three English prisons, *Prison Service Journal*, 209: 12–17.

Schmidt, B (2020) *Democratising democracy: Reimagining prisoners as active citizens through participatory governance*, PhD thesis, Institute of Criminology, University of Cambridge.

Solomon, E & Edgar, K (2004) *Having their say: The work of prisoner councils*. London: Prison Reform Trust.

4 Co-production with criminalised women

This chapter presents three separate case studies of co-production with women involved with the criminal justice system. Two are time-limited and prison-based: first, *Birds Eye View*, a podcast made with women from the Darwin Correctional Centre (Northern Territory, Australia), and second, the *Mothers' Project*, a collaborative research project with imprisoned mothers in Ireland. The final case study is of an ongoing community-based organisation, *Seeds of Affinity*, which supports and empowers women returning from prison to the community in Adelaide, South Australia. Across the adult correctional sector, women are in the minority. While the difference is most evident in prisons, where women make up around 7% of the population, even in community corrections, men outnumber women four to one (ABS, 2020). Of considerable concern is that women have been flagged over several years as being the fastest-growing group in the criminal justice sector (AIHW, 2020). In Australia, this trend seems to have been driven by the increasing imprisonment of Indigenous women (ALRC, 2018).

The impact of the feminist movement and feminist criminologists has been significant over recent decades, initially drawing attention to women as a largely invisible group in a system, and in more recent years, shifting this focus to advocating for equity and understanding gendered pathways into crime. To some extent, this has led to gender-responsive policy and practice in a range of Western settings, including Australia, Canada, the United Kingdom, and the United States (Hannah-Moffat, 2010), albeit largely confined to prisons (Burgess & Flynn, 2021). Such approaches seek to promote empowerment and self-efficacy, centralise an understanding of gender in crime, and provide programmes that seek to meet the distinctive needs of women, including mental health, victimisation, children, and substance use (Burgess & Flynn, 2021). While these approaches fit within a reformist agenda, overall, responses shaped by a gendered understanding of women and offending seem well aligned with co-production. In many ways, the collaborative practices and valuing of lived experience that

DOI: 10.4324/9780429328657-6

co-production emphasises have been fundamental to programmes with a feminist underpinning.

Birds Eye View

Birds Eye View[1] was a two-year podcast project, based at the Darwin Correctional Centre (DCC), led by producer Johanna Bell. The podcast featured 10 episodes, focusing on the lives of women in Sector Four of the DCC, a prison in which just 80 of the more than 1,000 prisoners are women. This case study is based on an interview with Johanna, and reference to her 2020 presentation[2] at the Australian podcast festival, Audiocraft, with Renae "Rocket" Bretherton, a woman who participated in the project. Johanna describes her first career as being in programme evaluation and social research, but after becoming disillusioned with this, she began experimenting with community storytelling. She says she wanted to

> help elevate authentic stories … over six years it led to uncovering areas that don't get heard. People, groups, communities that don't have conventional voice, which of course eventually led to the prison. And not only the broader prison, but the women's section of a men's prison. So, this is one of the least heard and least seen groups in the Northern Territory.

The Birds Eye View project ran from March 2018 to March 2020, when the podcast was released.

Birds Eye View started out as a community arts development project. It was funded by the Northern Territory Government, through the Department of Health, which recognised the power of storytelling as a public health tool (with some later funding from the Australia Council). It was funded under a broad spectrum of projects that seek to reduce alcohol-related harm. These projects typically target people from remote Aboriginal communities; as there is significant overrepresentation in the prison, a prison-based project was seen as a good fit. The original brief had been to run a programme called *Spun Stories* – a public storytelling event. Johanna's experience working cross-culturally, however, and with women from remote Aboriginal communities, suggested that capturing these stories via audio recording would be more appropriate. The latter, as well as giving editorial capacity, also provides more privacy in a prison space and a longer methodology for what she calls "slow storytelling". This brings a community cultural development framework, based on capacity building and empowerment. The brief was recrafted as a two-year audio storytelling project.

The project had three primary aims and intended audiences: (1) the wider public – to educate the community about the complexities of why people end up in prison, challenging some of the stereotypes; (2) women's families and communities – so they would hear stories of positive role models, but also of the negative consequences of actions, and that these would provide lessons for others walking a similar path; and (3) the women themselves – the primary audience. The aim for the women was to take part in a storytelling programme: participating in a series of workshops from recording techniques to interviewing, scripting, oral storytelling, as well as making the accompanying music (including vocals in the toilet!). The project involved a direct skills development aspect, but also the reflection that comes from "working deeply on your own narrative" (Johanna). This was particularly evident given the complexities in women's lives, including complex trauma and deep feelings of regret and disempowerment. The intention was that through personal storytelling, women would develop new skills, confidence, and the capacity to change.

Although this project had its origins in a government department, with external funding and producers, it was operationalised within a co-production approach, although described by Johanna in different terms: "We were calling it co-creation or collaboration". The project began with "co-conception" – where the focus and purpose of the podcast were developed by the group, with guiding questions providing a general compass. This helped to manage the

> messy, unhinged, unanchored, adrift feeling that comes with collaboration, when you're not holding the reins.
>
> (Johanna)

The project also involved women in co-development, co-editing, and finally co-promotion: "Typically, I [Johanna] don't present unless somebody co-presents with me". It is clear, however, that these labels sit and fit more easily now, and are more meaningful, two years later, when the shape and outcomes of the project are clear. Women were initially sceptical that the project would truly be collaborative until this was actually experienced. Rocket specifically notes the experience of editorial control over her own story.

This project encapsulates many elements from across the co-production spectrum (Weaver *et al.* 2019), though not staff recruitment and selection or governance and administration. What is evident, however, is that much of this is informal peer-teaching or peer-sharing:

> people would become skilled, with say, the microphones, and then would go out into the yard and they'd be recording. And ... then passing

those skills on to somebody who was less confident, who was next to them.

While this project sought in part to challenge the stereotypes of women in prison by hearing women's voices, it was also seen to carry perceived risks, specifically the risk to a government institution of "allowing" women in prison to narrate their own stories, and for these to be available via a public podcast, in an election year. Johanna describes the weight of this responsibility for women's stories to be heard as being "unimaginably heavy", with a sense of the project being vulnerable to the whims of "someone at the top [getting] cold feet".

Structural support is evident in what has helped Birds Eye View to be successfully co-produced. Time and pre-existing groundwork in the specific prison setting were two vital elements. Framing the project as long-term enabled relationships to be built with the women over time. Johanna describes the first three to four months being spent building rapport and trust before any work was done with recording equipment. This is highly pertinent in a prison setting as this is "not a place where people trust easily". Physical space was also pertinent. In this project, having access to the library within the prison – with no cameras – created a safer space for women to talk. The long-term nature of the project also provided temporal space to work around people's individual challenges (e.g. not being "in the right headspace on the day you were there ... but there the following week") as well as the systemic challenges of the prison setting, including lockdowns or women being required to participate in other activities and appointments.

Establishing relationships with staff was also key, building on the "lineage [at DCC] of working with artists inside the prison system", specifically the successful *Prison Songs* programme. Working within the system, but from an outsider perspective, is also seen to have had some benefits:

> As an external contractor I was able to operate on terms and at a pace that's actually at odds with the way the bureaucracy operates. It allows you a degree of freedom and allows you to take risks that a government department cannot take.

A range of intersecting and multi-layered factors were a challenge to the co-production of Birds Eye View. Structural factors played a part, including staffing changes at both the prison and commissioner level, which required "a lot of extra work in re-educating people at the top about the project", where innovation such as this can be framed as risky, particularly, as noted above, in an election year. But challenges at the individual level were also evident, both for the women and the project producers. Working as an independent producer, with no supervision, listening to stories of trauma brought with it burnout. Rocket also reminds us of the additional hurdle that must be traversed by those in prison when asked to contribute, and share ideas and opinions – to participate: that the very context does not encourage people to make decisions for themselves, and in fact works against women having control over their own lives.

This project has now concluded, with some powerful lessons for others and for future projects, mostly about pre-empting likely difficulties. From project planning in a risk-averse environment, having documented safeguards in place, to ensure that irrespective of any "changing of the guard or the changing of sentiment, that the promises made ... [will] be upheld", to understanding that co-production is both costly and beneficial for those participating. From a worker perspective, being able to share power, as noted earlier, as well as being open to challenges:

> Definitely get ready to be uncomfortable, because I think if you're not uncomfortable you're not doing collaboration properly.
>
> (Johanna)

Understanding that co-production can be both an opportunity and a burden, and that collaboration can involve a range of levels of activity:

> Not everybody has to have the same level of understanding, but everyone has to have enough understanding to move forward together.

Johanna's key suggestions are insightful: allowing time to move slowly and build trust; creating opportunities for participants and team members to have supervision or psychological support, ideally working in tandem with a counselling service; and importantly, involving more First Nations team members. And a challenge to us all: how to capture the small but seismic changes that occur and ripple through a woman's life and social network.

The Mothers' Project

The Mothers' Project (so named by the participants) is an ongoing project coordinated by Dr Sinead O'Malley. It began as a UNESCO-funded PhD study examining the lives and experiences of mothers in prison in Ireland. Project participants continue to work collaboratively to share the findings, conduct training, and do further research, to advocate for women in prison; they are supported by an informal network of activists and related professionals. This case study is based on an interview with Sinead, as well as some reference to her PhD thesis (O'Malley 2016). She came to this work with a master's degree in social work (MSW) and lived experience of the criminal justice system. This project had its origins in a previous study that Sinead had done as part of her MSW, where she interviewed key prison and criminal justice staff. In completing that project, she says she discovered that maternal imprisonment was an issue that had not been considered previously in Ireland, and more particularly had not been considered as a child welfare issue, from the perspective of women, as Sinead described:

> So, I applied to do the PhD but I knew at that point that I wanted to involve the mums, that I wanted it to be a participatory study, that we looked at what the systems knew and didn't know but we had never really asked the direct voices of the women in prison themselves about their experiences.

The primary aim of this study was to explore how women in prison in Ireland experienced the informal institution of motherhood and performed their mothering role whilst incarcerated: to give visibility to their children and supports. While considerable research had been done in recent decades on maternal incarceration, Sinead's aim was to do this in a very specific and participatory way, to redress the obvious imbalance and lack of voice from marginalised mothers:

> I suppose within all of that, being an ex-prisoner and a mother, I couldn't have imagined doing it any other way, I couldn't have imagined doing the study without direct voices of the women, giving them an opportunity.

The overall project is not described as co-production, mainly because as the researcher, Sinead says, *she* identified the issues of concern and instigated the project – "I knew there were gaps" – rather than the focus being co-identified and peer-led. Her assessment is that this approach, not from the grassroots up, brought a "power dynamic. No matter how much you get rid of it there's a power dynamic". However, each of the two prison sites in which the study was conducted had a participatory consultation group of women "who were involved in everything", and Sinead describes elements of co-production being evident, in more nuanced ways, throughout the project:

> There were three different layers of participation … there was stuff that I brought or the system brought, there was stuff that we worked on together and there was stuff that was completely participant-led.

For example, after she developed her idea for a research project, this was presented to women in prison for approval. This type of consultative participation was also evident in processes such as constructing the study's consent form. While the form was developed by the Irish Prison Service (IPS), it was taken to the group of women for input on "how it's worded and make sure everybody understands it". Other aspects of the study were more women-led, such as the development of specific questions in the questionnaire and the voiceovers for these (the study used a computer-based questionnaire where questions could be accessed and listened to verbally). The design of a recruitment poster, as well as the content of a computer game provided at the end of the questionnaire, as a fun way to finish up, was completely led by participants. The study findings were and are presented collaboratively, with the women co-presenting in prison settings and at community events.

A range of individual, structural, and temporal factors assisted the implementation of this project. Having the study funded by UNESCO, and sitting within an existing family research centre, with a specific focus on "engaging with research that makes a difference and participatory research really echoes that philosophy", provided validation for the project and its approach. Sinead also described the context as being "ready", perhaps compared to "10 years ago maybe it wouldn't have happened". At an organisational level, a supportive prison environment – notably staff championing the project – was invaluable. A prison governor (who had participated in the initial MSW study) paved the way, supported by individual prison staff with their own "individual interest" in the project. This institutional support meant that Sinead was granted unfettered access to the prison:

> I was gifted power by these keys, where I could work freely and walk freely between different sections of the prison where the women couldn't go. Actually it was one of the women who said it to me, she said 'Jesus, Sinead, look how things have turned around for you, holding those keys.'

Prison officer involvement was also acknowledged, as was women's participation, with a certificate from UNESCO and the IPS. Sinead's lived experience was also seen to aid the process:

> so the women would know I'd been an ex-prisoner, and I think that helped them relax a little bit … [seeing that] 'she's one of us'.

She also described the importance of fun:

> The amount of fun we had – this is where the laughter comes in … it was so good.

Not unexpectedly, a range of structural factors also hindered the process. At a practical level, when organisational support – again specifically staffing – was absent in the prison system, this affected the capacity to work collaboratively. Sinead reports that subsequent to the Mothers' Project, she has been back in the prison doing follow-up work, but that "it hasn't worked as fluidly, because I suppose the officers who were due to support me haven't had the same level of interest". The lack of understanding from broader systems and structures of the "costs" involved in co-production is also a hindrance. Actual financial costs are another key aspect. Sinead described being proactive, seeking, and winning

> a number of different funding streams, small funding to support the participatory process. Had I not fought for that funding, fought and applied for that funding it wouldn't have been possible, I couldn't afford it. ... Had I not done that, there would be no Mothers' Project, as much as they want participatory work and a participatory study.

The financial needs of this project also flowed onto Sinead as the sole, student, facilitator:

> The financial strain on our family was really hard because I had to fork everything out, before I got it back. That didn't end for me when the project ended although it did for the university when the project ended.

She emphasised the need to consider the ongoing costs associated with research once data collection is concluded:

> I felt there was a disjuncture there between dissemination processes, and for that fact that I ringfenced the pot of money to continue dissemination after, that would never have happened.

A lack of understanding of and attention to the emotional implications and costs for women and those facilitating co-produced projects can also impede such work. With regard to participants,

> people invest so much in participatory work. ... I am unsure how that can stop just because the PhD ends. ... Do we not have a duty to support those who were instrumental in designing the recommendations?

But Sinead also importantly notes the implications for those facilitating such projects:

> anybody, and me included, who reaches the prison gates, arrives with their backpack of trauma and whatever that looks like. So I was obviously revisiting some of that stuff … it is a really, really difficult process and then as an ex-prisoner and a mother leaving my children, going to a prison, all that kind of emotion with other mothers who are separated from their kids, exhausting, absolutely exhausting. …. In research I don't think there's a very good structure around researcher counselling and support. … I engaged in [independent] research counselling to aid my reflexivity process.

Even with this support, the emotional labour which Sinead carried is evident.

She is clear that collaborative work benefits from being grounded in mutual interdependence: "I wouldn't have done it without the women, and they probably wouldn't have done it without me, to be fair". She is also of the view that working from this standpoint brings the capacity to generate different knowledge, and that if it had been done in a different way:

> I don't think it would have been the same. I don't think it would have been the same study, it wouldn't have been the same findings. … I don't know if as many women would have got involved if it hadn't been done the way it was done.

Sinead also emphasised the need for a longer-term view, alongside adequate funding, to ensure ethical practice, because:

> participatory work … is actually quite dangerous if you don't foresee the future within that. So, you're looking at supporting people and ethically supporting people thereafter around how they engaged in their emotions, actually, to help you with this project and to help themselves or to help their future group and yet then the project is over and it finishes because there's no money.

From Sinead's perspective, abandoning the support provided to people and groups once a project ends is dangerously unethical.

Seeds of Affinity

Seeds of Affinity[3] (Seeds) is a not-for-profit support service for women exiting prison, based in Adelaide, South Australia. It provides group activities, runs a social enterprise (making skincare products and gourmet foods), and provides guest speakers at a range of settings, such as universities or church groups. It was established in 2006, with the aim of women working together to create a community of support for other women leaving prison and their children. Seeds seeks to challenge and educate the community about related issues as a way of addressing stigma, advocating for the needs and rights of these women in the social and political sphere. This case study is based on an interview with Fiona Woollard, a member of Seeds Inc., and organisational materials. Fiona – now a volunteer/support worker – first got involved with Seeds as a woman leaving prison. She says she was:

> encouraged to come [but knew I could] leave if I don't like it. You're told in prison so much what you have to do. So, I guess to be given that freedom, it was my choice, and so I took that and I never looked back.

Seeds grew out of a working relationship between Anna, a parole officer, and Linda, a woman who had been involved with the corrections system. Fiona describes Seeds being established in response to a need these two women had identified together:

> that many women ... were falling through the cracks ... not being accepted into community centres. ... They felt like they were being judged. ... It was something that they'd seen that there needed to be – a space for women to come together and feel a sense of community, feel a sense of togetherness and a sense of belonging. ... They saw that need and so discussed about what they could do. Basically, it started by having women come together to have a shared lunch and just share experiences, a small group, which grew from there.

Fiona describes the aims of Seeds as being to "empower women. To empower criminalised women. To try and help them gain an identity other than being criminalised women". Seeds does this by offering regular support groups, meals, and discussion, but they also offer the opportunity for women to contribute back to the community, by participating in making soaps and other products, which are sold to support the organisation. Attendees also make "prison packs". Fiona explained that:

> when you go to prison here, you're not issued with a deodorant or a soap or shampoo or conditioner ... quite often women will go into prison with no money. So they go two weeks without actually receiving any hygiene things, apart from a toothbrush and toothpaste.

Making these packs allows Seeds and those involved to "contribute back to the women in prison". Seeds has been a collaborative venture since its inception. Women are involved as members:

> Basically, Seeds is run by and for women, criminalised women ... [the] majority of the decisions and things are made by the women for the women ... volunteers take a very back step when decisions need to be made.

Fiona described this approach as co-production:

> because the women make the choices. Anything that is asked ... it'll always be brought to the table and it'll be, 'Okay, this is what's being proposed. What do we think?' And it'll be left to the women to have discussion and decide it. ... Whatever happens within Seeds it's always discussed and decided on by all.

Seeds' approach to co-production is spread across the continuum, from consultation and feedback, in "the discussions that we have at the table", through to representation and engagement of women in speaking engagements, presenting at forums and workshops, and ultimately shaping and designing the way the group will go forward.

Support at multiple levels has aided Seeds to co-produce services. While not described by Fiona as a feminist organisation, a strong ideological framework is evident, of women voluntarily connecting with and supporting other women, in a holistic and flexible way. This is actioned through personal connection and commitment: "It's done out of love and passion and they're just driven". But commitment also brings a cost:

> Linda has her phone on 24 hours a day. She's answering calls through the night. She deals with those situations, and she does this all on a volunteer basis, and has done since the organisation started.

Having Anna, an experienced corrections officer, as a champion and advocate inside the system is invaluable. However, there is a fine line between the advocacy initiated by Seeds and the boundaries enforced by the correctional system, making it challenging to negotiate the expectations of this statutory agency. For Seeds, remaining somewhat outside of "the system" has allowed the organisation to retain its independence and its approach:

> You take the funding, you've got to abide by certain rules and obligations and meet certain criteria and KPIs and that type of thing.

... We won't necessarily change a way of doing something if we don't think it's beneficial for the women, first and foremost ... We don't want to have to fit people into boxes to meet KPIs.

Yet accessing scarce funding is acknowledged to be required for longer-term sustainability and the growth of the organisation: "you don't take the funding, well then, you're limited with what you can do. It's a real balancing act", with ongoing grant applications consuming much Board time and energy. There are clearly mixed feelings about relationships with the formal service system. Seeds describes significant periods where "we operate without any funding and sustain ourselves through social enterprises and charity events, [achievable] as we have put time and energy into building a community of volunteers".

The need for a safe space for women exiting prison to come together and work together is key to this approach, to "ensure that everyone knows that it's a safe space for everyone and people have their vulnerabilities", with clear and shared values and boundaries. For this group, Fiona is of the view that given the prevalence of histories of family violence, a women's only space is important.

Notes

1 https://www.birdseyeviewpodcast.net/.
2 https://www.audiocraft.com.au/audiocraft-podcast-season-5-ep-6
3 https://seedsofaffinity.org/

References

Australian Bureau of Statistics (ABS) (2020) *Corrective services Australia – March quarter 2021*. Canberra: ABS.

Australian Institute of Health and Welfare (AIHW) (2020) *The health and welfare of women in Australia's prisons*. Canberra: AIHW.

Australian Law Reform Commission (ALRC) (2018) *Pathways to justice: Inquiry into the incarceration rate of aboriginal and Torres Strait Islander peoples*. Report 133. Queensland: ARLC.

Burgess, A & Flynn, C (2021) Maternal mental illness: Mediating women's trajectory through the Victorian criminal justice system, *Women & Criminal Justice*, https://doi.org/10.1080/08974454.2021.1942399

Hannah-Moffat, K (2010) Sacrosanct or flawed: Risk, accountability and gender-responsive penal politics, *Current Issues in Criminal Justice*, 22(2): 193–215.

O'Malley, S (2016) *Motherhood, mothering and the Irish prison system*, PhD thesis, National University of Ireland, Galway, Ireland.

Weaver, B, Lightowler, C & Moodie, K (2019) Inclusive justice: Co-producing change – A practical guide to service user involvement in community justice. CYCJ, Scotland.

5 Practitioner perspectives on co-production

As outlined in Chapter 1, criminal justice is a large and complex structure comprising many overlapping systems. Practitioner roles vary widely and include casework, case management, group work, education, counselling, and mentoring, with a range of disciplines involved in providing services (Trotter, 2018; Turner 2010) in both community and statutory settings. A focus on risk management characterises both adult corrections and youth justice, with young people becoming "special targets" in an increasingly punitive, managerial project (Maruna & King, 2008: 129). Given the widespread uptake of the Risk–Needs–Responsivity model (Andrews & Bonta, 2010), it is perhaps unsurprising that psychologists now have a key role to play in the delivery of clinical services, bringing a focus on individual pathology and "offender rehabilitation". Overall, however, there is a lack of consensus about the training and qualification requirements for workers in corrections and youth justice (Stout, 2017). This, arguably, correlates with the lack of value placed on workers' knowledge and skills, as well as outcomes for service users. In youth justice, Healy (2016) contends, professionals, including "social workers have been sidelined ... because they challenge inappropriate, ineffective and inhumane practices". Stout (2017: 55) similarly observes that youth justice in Australia is "moving increasingly away from social work" and its foundational human rights and social justice values.

In this chapter, we present two different examples of social workers working within the criminal justice system, and co-producing knowledge about criminal justice, but in very different ways. *Straight Talking* is a place-based peer-mentoring programme for people leaving prison. It was conceived and driven by Claire Seppings, who has extensive experience of working in and around prisons as a social worker, naturopath, and as a former partner of someone repeatedly imprisoned over many years. Claire applied her professional and personal experience to the study of the rehabilitative role of ex-prisoners as peer mentors, under a Churchill

DOI: 10.4324/9780429328657-7

Fellowship (Seppings, 2015). The *Youth Justice* case study centres on Tim Warton's engagement with imprisoned young men, exploring their narratives of the development of criminal identity, as part of his doctoral research (Warton, 2020). As a senior Youth Justice practitioner, Tim brought to this research several years' experience as a social worker and counsellor, and skills, in direct practice with youth and adults in the justice system, including with young people who have sexually offended. Common to both case studies and their protagonists, then, is a professional qualification in social work and an underlying orientation to genuinely rehabilitative work, that is, helping people to change their lives.

Straight Talking

Straight Talking is a peer-mentoring programme trialled (in 2017–2019) with men leaving a medium-security prison and returning to live in the Geelong area, a regional city in Victoria, Australia. The programme – offered by Deakin University with philanthropic funding and in collaboration with the Victorian Department of Justice and Community Safety – is based on Claire's Churchill Fellowship (Seppings, 2015). The Deakin University project, led by Professor Joe Graffam, involved the planning, development, and implementation of the programme, including recruitment, training, and support of mentors, as well as recruitment of mentees, and facilitation of these relationships. An evaluation was undertaken, however, at the time of writing, the report was not yet publicly available. This case study is based on an interview with Claire, the mastermind, developer, and coordinator of the project. Claire is a social worker and criminal justice consultant. She is Chair of the Victorian Custody Reference Group (VCRG), 2012 recipient of the VCRG's Access to Justice Award, and a member of the Women's Correctional Services Advisory Committee.

This project is the culmination of a professional and personal journey for Claire, spanning several years and drawing on a range of experiences, relationships, ideas, and interest groups. The groundwork for the programme began in the early 2000s, as Claire, with a justice portfolio in her Commonwealth Government social work role, began attending the Reintegration Puzzle conference. This annual event brings together people who have an interest in supporting community reintegration after prison. Claire presented on such prison work at these conferences over the years and developed working relationships and shared interests with Professor Joe Graffam and Jenny Crosbie from Deakin University, which was to be instrumental in the development of Straight Talking. Claire also had in-depth personal experience of prison, with a previous partner cycling in and out of the system. A critical personal moment came when as a conference participant she perceived:

> they're all talking about families of prisoners, and it hit a chord; I'm thinking 'You're talking about me' ... But back then it was like the shame thing of that kind of world, so it was definite to keep that completely separate.

Claire felt the significance of her personal experience, albeit remaining a hidden victim of crime. It was not until her then partner's third incarceration during their relationship, and he said while they walked around the visit centre garden, "I don't know how to be straight", that she realised that although "I'd known him now for probably about 15 years ... we couldn't be further apart ... we are like two separate beings." This sparked the start of her thinking about learning from those who had also experienced prison. Claire recalls "it took about a year to develop that whole idea [for the Churchill Fellowship]". This time also allowed for the canvassing of ideas, support, and feedback from a range of stakeholders, notably ex-prisoners, and decision-makers within the correctional system. The Fellowship report formed the foundation of the Straight Talking programme. The goal of this project was to provide a:

> through-the-gate peer mentoring program, which meant we were going to have ex-prisoners going back into the prison to connect with, build a relationship with a guy in prison who wanted that support ... [This was to be provided] one-on-one, and then they would follow them out again and continue that support, as long as they wanted it.

The aim was to connect mentors and mentees about 6 months prior to release and to provide formal support up to 12 months post-release. The location for the pilot was based on place-based funding, and existing evidence about the needs in that location: "some of those men are going back to those postcodes that have the highest rate of crime or imprisonment and recidivism or whatever".

Across the life of this project, co-production was a fundamental principle, although how it was enacted varied. The foundation of the programme was constructed via learning gleaned – via the Fellowship – directly from those who had previously been incarcerated and were using this experience to support others. The design and development of the specific Straight Talking model drew on specialist input from both ex-prisoners and those currently involved with the prison or community corrections system. Ex-prisoners acted as consultants, presenting and modelling the idea of peer mentoring to both prisoners and prison staff. These consultants, along with the lead peer and other mentors, "became part of the ongoing working group that we'd meet in the prison". The current prisoners, parolees, and those on community corrections orders gave their opinions and feedback via "the prisoner focus group, [and] the questionnaires that came back". The delivery of the programme itself was co-produced. An ex-prisoner was sought and employed as the lead peer mentor to "support the volunteer mentors that we would bring on board". This lead mentor was also involved in interviewing and selecting suitable volunteers for the programme.

Solid and multi-layered foundations were key to the programme, from its basis in the Churchill Fellowship findings – learning from other programmes in the United Kingdom, Europe, and the United States – to Claire's own experiences, and the groundwork to get key supporters on board. Claire's professional experience meant that she understood how bureaucracies worked and what support was needed to drive and sustain innovation. Fostering support at a managerial level within the prison system from the outset gave the project credibility with general staff and helped resolve practical challenges. One major problem, considered by many at the outset to be an insurmountable problem, was access: "it just seemed everyone was saying, 'What a great idea, but you'll never get them [formerly imprisoned men] back into the prison'".

Sustained managerial support was crucial to resolving such issues. But ongoing attention to "maintaining relationships" was important more widely. This included working with community stakeholders, partners, and service users. As project coordinator, Claire convened a working group to collaboratively develop the programme, comprising members from the prison and community corrections and people with lived experience of prison. The group developed guidelines, protocols, and procedures, which were presented to the project's inter-agency reference group for review and endorsement. Claire describes her personal experience as central to her work. Her ability to recognise and use this knowledge has been influenced by timing, with discourse about lived experience in criminal justice becoming more open in the past five years or so. She is clear that "before that I don't think anyone would have been ready ... I think people get it now".

The additional challenges of doing co-production in criminal justice, in the community, are evident. The reference group at times had to manage risk, and perceptions of risk, to make decisions about the boundaries of the project, and who would make a suitable mentor. Not everyone is suited to being a mentor or mentee and – primarily due to the small number of people in the trial, and its pilot nature – some groups were excluded, such as convicted sex offenders and those on parole. The issue of how much time should have elapsed since imprisonment before someone could be a mentor was also considered. Based on learning from existing programmes, and feedback from prisoners and staff, they decided that this would be assessed on a case-by-case basis, considering issues such as:

> If ... you've still got to go to so many whatever appointments a week, are you ready to support somebody else, if you've still got to do a lot for yourself? ... [What have you] been doing in that time [since prison], and your ability to reflect on yourself, to demonstrate that you're ready for this ... [ensuring that] they're still not too close to criminal activity, addiction, all of that ... but you still want – partly for your own recovery – to give back and help others.

Despite the challenges, Claire is of the view that she would not do anything differently: "We've actually done everything that we said we would do". She does note one area for consideration going forward: to recognise the emotional work and the toll this can take. People working or volunteering as peer mentors can find themselves "reliv[ing] [their] own experience", and in need of clinical supervision. Claire notes that although she "had years of experience of it – being a social worker, and supervising and managing staff – this needs someone, who knows that world", who can assist in helping peers find balance in "sharing their life experience, and putting their heart out ... and [being aware that you may] expose yourself too". She cautions that in co-production we need to ensure that we are not just using people, and to know there is "a level of support [that] needs to be given after that". This includes thinking about supporting people's careers, not just harnessing peers "to do the dirty work, as ... the volunteers at the grassroots".

Claire's drive to reform the prison system through the expertise of those who have lived it continues through her work within various justice networks and as an Inaugural Policy Impact Program Fellow for 2020.

Youth Justice

Dr Timothy Warton is a social worker and Senior Project Officer (Practice) for Youth Justice in NSW, where has worked in various direct practice and clinical management roles for more than a decade. He also runs Dragonfly Counselling, Consultancy & Supervision service, which specialises in child and adolescent problematic sexualised behaviours. Tim completed a practice-based doctoral study where he interviewed and analysed the narratives of 20 young males in NSW youth detention centres to explore the development of a criminal identity, from their own perspectives (Warton, 2020). He explored how the young men see themselves, the groups they feel they fit into, and the way they believe others see them in relation to crime and criminality. This case study is based on an interview with Tim, where he reflects on his experiences of conducting this research.

Notably, it was only through the course of the interview that Tim decided his study constituted "co- production", as this is not a term he was previously familiar with:

> Co-production and co-design are not terms being used in youth justice – never heard them before in my life in youth justice, but it's really easy to get language into the bureaucracy – all you have to do is just say the terms in a meeting [and that] all the cool kids are saying 'co- production' now. And then everyone else wants to say it. [They] may or may not know the meaning. It happens all the time – hilarious.

Tim recognised his approach as "partnering" or "collaborating" with young people to understand an issue from their point of view:

> Partnering – exactly what I'm saying. I'm fairly confident that I was able to establish relationships that were reciprocal, that allowed the young person to talk, that gave them the power of expertise over their own lives. You just provide them the space to give their narrative and it just starts coming out. Just to encourage the fact that they own their own experience; they're the ones that are the experts on it. In retrospect, after this discussion, I feel like it was co-production. I could have had a section in my methodology about the co-production of knowledge.

Taking a "grounded approach" to the research, Tim tried to avoid superimposing existing schemas or ideas onto the young persons' narratives:

> If you're going to focus on co-production, it needs to be a grounded approach. You're just totally open to whatever happens … and you need to make sense of it afterwards.

Tim felt "acutely aware" that beyond the collaborative and dialogical nature of the interview, it would be he who would interpret and "apply meaning to that knowledge". He asked two academics with similar practice backgrounds to review sections of the interview transcripts and found they arrived at "very similar interpretations" to his own. Tim felt confident that this process did not unduly dilute the young people's voices, partly because his professional practice skills and experience ensured he had initially understood the young persons' meanings:

I had to use a lot of basic one-to-one counselling skills, right? 'Am I hearing you right? Is this what you're saying?' I found those sorts of skills really helped.

Tim felt that his professional practice skills and experience also helped him to effectively engage and establish trust with young people, as necessary precursors for knowledge co-production:

The interview skills you need, on reflection, I just took for granted. Co-producing data with a young person can be really tricky, because you're talking about, particularly in the criminal justice system, things that are highly charged. There's lots of shame and embarrassment around these experiences … particularly with sex offenders, right? You got to create an environment that, you know, you can talk about having sex with your stepsister and not feel judged. I think I took those skills for granted. Now if you've been in academia your whole life I would imagine that's really nerve-wracking, I would think that's really hard to do.

Given his knowledge and expertise was quite specific to youth justice, Tim added that he would find it "tricky" to simply transfer this to another field, such as aged care. Nevertheless, Tim described feeling like a "phony" or "complete fraud" as a researcher. He felt that his ideas of truth and reality were too straightforward:

the stuff that I think is true, can't be true; there must be something I'm missing, some sort of academic mystery that I'm not getting, because I felt like I was just doing some sort of heavily modified pre-sentence interviews, I felt like it was my normal work, and I felt like I was understanding things in the 'wrong' way, I felt like I was understanding them like, just like a normal clinician or something like that.

Tim appears to be alluding to similarities in the skills and competencies required to effectively conduct and interpret an interview with young people for research or assessment purposes. He noted that he could have written a court report with the interview data, but that instead he had "to try and turn this into meaning and represent what they're saying just in its purest form, so other people understand it". He kept asking himself, "am I doing this right?"

Tim noted the significance of language as a facilitator and barrier to the mutual understanding necessary for co-producing knowledge. He described how young people use language embedded with their own nuanced meanings. For example, they used the words "bitch", "flop", and "buckled" to denote weakness in a person, rather than the usual meanings associated with these terms. For Tim, it was important not to assume that common terms hold a shared meaning or to interpret these terms from a perspective other than the young person's:

> I got to the point where I was thinking, being a linguist would help here. ... All these words that mean different things and that are so easy – particularly for academics – to look through with our own very strong, bubbled little lenses. But the young people have no relationship with this – they don't understand that. Our lenses are important, but we've just got to take them all off for a bit and use the young person's lens ... you really need to understand the meaning the young person is trying to get across.

Tim also noted the importance of relationships and the relevance of power dynamics that operate at various levels in the criminal justice system and as part of the process of knowledge co-production. He discussed, for example, the nature of relationships between universities and government departments, which he argues for the most part "are not good". Academics are seen by government administrators as "investigative journalists", intent on exposing poor practices and blowing things up, so the response from government departments is to be "really cagey about what they give academics access to". Tim argues that universities need to invest a lot more in relationships with government departments, as these are key to knowledge co-production:

> If we're going to co-produce, we need to nail the relationships. The universities and the departments need to have a bit of a group hug.

He further suggests there "may be an air of elitism or lack of front-line experience" for some academic researchers, which acts as a barrier to forming relationships with department administrators and staff, as well as research participants:

> I think potentially, academic interviewers if they don't have experience in the field need to spend some time honing their interview skills – and maybe that's about frontline work.

A key element for Tim, in developing trust to co-produce knowledge with children and young people, is paying attention to – and working to mitigate – the multiple, inherent power imbalances. However, the explicit symbols of power that are evident in the criminal justice system work to undermine this at an individual level:

> Everything comes down to a meaningful connection between the person in power – the state representative – and the young person. But to do that is hard depending on your context.

Tim adds that although knowledge co-production is essentially an equalising process, the levels of responsibility inherent in this are not equal, particularly when the relationship involves children and young people:

> With the emphasis on co-production, that means we as adults have to do a lot of work to make sure that it is collaborative, because we are the ones with the power, we are the ones with the education and all that sort of stuff, so we have to do the work to make sure it's collaborative.

Also, the approach would need to vary across the life course to respond effectively to the child and young person's changing developmental stage and needs:

> It's on us [as adults] to do the sorts of things I did in the research – extrapolate the meaning of what they're saying, without the onus of responsibility for change or accurate articulation on the young person. It needs to be slow and long-winded and they need to be able to make mistakes and not be judged. It takes a lot of skill. You can't just walk in and ask, 'What do you want?' That's a train wreck. If it's co-design it needs to be exactly that. [Yes], a discourse, a narrative, ongoing dialogue.

Tim believes it is possible to meaningfully engage young people in co-creating a reimagined youth justice system, but that it would not look much like the current system. Instead, it would be much more informal and focused on ensuring a "good life" for the young people. Young people typically like to make friends and may suggest, for example, relaxing rules about associating with other young people in the youth justice office waiting areas. However, the rules are in place to avoid younger children and adolescents or those with less offending experience mixing with and being influenced by older, more experienced, sophisticated, or predatory young people involved in offending behaviour.

> I'm thinking about the balance in co-production. This is co-production, this isn't just their production, so we'd have to as adults consider things they wouldn't consider – and you do the same thing with children everywhere. You don't let children play on the road, even though they

might really want to, but you can explain to them that this is dangerous and they say, 'Oh yeah, ok, I'll play on the grass'. I don't think young people want to see that [approach] go, because someone's got to take the authority and [if it isn't a pro-social adult] it's probably going to be a really antisocial young person.

Tim noted that this is evident in youth detention centres:

Youth workers in centres who are less engaged and lackadaisical and don't take that adult, leadership role, [it's] almost visceral, you can feel it: kids are far more anxious, I'm going to stand against a wall, I'm not feeling safe, put a mouthguard in, I'm not feeling good about this situation, there's going to be a fight ... but when you have the 'effective parent' on the unit, it's a different feel – people are relaxed, they know where the leadership is, they know where the safe space is – it's not about power and control, it's about authority and safety. Authority that says 'I'm here to help and keep you safe and maintain the rules; I'm here to help maintain order'.

As with any research with children and young people, and particularly in the criminal justice context, gaining access to research participants was a key issue for Tim. He required ethics clearance for his study and acknowledges that his insider-researcher status helped facilitate this. However, he had to consult with and to some extent rely on the youth justice workers in custody to provide him with access to the young people. While this was mostly unproblematic, some workers suggested particular young people for Tim to interview, noting they were "easy". Other workers suggested young people who were known to be "challenging", expecting the young person would not participate in the interview, in an apparent effort to undermine the research process.

One challenge conducting research in a youth detention centre, Tim noted, was the lack of anonymity for both him and the participants.

They all knew me ... I couldn't hide, I couldn't – anonymity was so hard. ... I'd go in sort of six months later, for work, and they'd want to have another chat.

However, it helped that the young people were literally a "captive audience":

I think that helped, absolutely, and the incentive helped ... Socks. Big-ticket item, right? Nike socks, ankle socks. ... It had the little tick on it, which was important. ... Incentives mean more in custody, and there's nowhere near as much need to organise and set appointment times and things that young people in particular are terrible at. It's harder in the community for any adolescent to keep times – it's harder for adolescents in general.

Tim reflected on the young people's motivations for agreeing to talk to him and concluded that in addition to their desire for the formal incentives, the young people enjoyed the opportunity to get out of the usual custodial centre routines. That is, to sit and talk with Tim in a separate room when everyone else was in "lockdown". There seemed to be an element of "beating the system" that was perhaps a bit subversive – "especially if they didn't like the youth officers on shift". Nonetheless, Tim also felt that the young people were motivated by a desire to tell their story and make it better for "the younger boys" or those who come after them:

> It was made quite clear that they could just take the incentive and run if they wanted to – 'You don't have to be here, you're not going to hurt my feelings; it's all good.' And they just stuck around. Once their – once the engine was started – they were on and on and on, they seemed quite keen to give me their story and effect change for those that come after them.

He speculated that this may have been influenced by their incarceration context:

> I did also feel like there was kind of a desperation to get these really clear messages that they had, out. In a more voluntary situation, I feel like there wouldn't be that same eagerness to get that message out, it's almost like [they were saying] 'I'm being oppressed, help me!'

Tim further speculated that the young people might have viewed him as:

> a potential ally, against the youth officers, or against the shift supervisors ... on reflection ... I felt like an official visitor a bit. I don't know how that affected what we produced.

These are the tensions for anti-oppressive practitioners confronting the power inherent in their role.

References

Andrews, D & Bonta, J (2010) *The psychology of criminal conduct*. New York: Taylor & Francis.

Healy, K (2016) AASW opinion – NT juvenile justice: Hard work needed now, not another word- fest, Australian Association of Social Workers. July 27. https://www.aasw.asn.au/news-media/2016

Maruna, S & King, A (2008) Giving up on the young, *Current Issues in Criminal Justice*, 20(1): 129–134.

Seppings, C (2015) *To study the rehabilitative role of ex-prisoners/offenders as peer mentors in reintegration models*. Churchill Fellowship Report, The Winston Churchill Memorial Trust, Australia.

Stout, B (2017) *Community justice in Australia: Developing knowledge, skills and values for working with offenders in the community*. Crows Nest: Allen & Unwin.

Trotter, C (2018) Criminal justice: Extending the social work focus. In M Alston, S McCurdy & J McKinnon (Eds.), *Social work: Fields of practice*, 3rd edn. South Melbourne, VIC: Oxford University Press, pp. 196–209.

Turner, S (2010) Case management in corrections: Evidence, issues and challenges. In C Trotter, P Raynor & F McNeill (Eds.), *Offender supervision: New directions in theory, research and practice*. London: Routledge, pp. 344–366.

Warton, TJ (2020) *The development of a criminal identity amongst adolescent males*. PhD thesis, Monash University, Melbourne.

6 Keeping on Country

Research in criminal justice is often conducted to produce evidence about ways to reduce recidivism. Yet, while Aboriginal and Torres Strait Islander peoples are overrepresented in criminalised populations (as administrative data and the lived experience of affected communities tells us), rarely are First Nations peoples asked what *they* think would work to address this problem. Even though Australia (as a party to the Declaration on the Rights of Indigenous People) ostensibly supports principles of self-determination, research is too often conducted *on* – and services delivered *to* – not *with* or *by* Aboriginal and Torres Strait Islander peoples. One exception is the *Keeping on Country* project based in two remote communities in the Gulf country of Far North Queensland, a project that arose out of the work of the Doomadgee Woolbubinya Wellbeing Centre and the Mornington Island Kalngkurr Wellbeing Centre.

Commissioned as part of the Federal Government's "Breaking the Cycle" initiative, the focus of the project was on developing strategies to address high rates of recidivism in the two communities. Though described as a research project, Keeping on Country goes beyond research: it builds on a community-identified problem of people from Mornington Island (Kunhanhaa) and Doomadgee being imprisoned far from home and then finding it hard to get back to their communities. This problem was framed as a "recidivism" and "reintegration" problem, in correctional terms, which instigated a federally funded pilot programme to address the issue. The programme and the research that aimed to track its progress and describe its outcomes were designed according to co-production principles. In this way, from the outset, the project relied on relationships between people inside and outside the local communities working together, in partnership. These are the elements explored in this case study.[1]

Mornington Island (Kunhanhaa) and Doomadgee are two distinct but closely related communities. Mornington Island lies 28 kilometres off the coast in the south of the Gulf of Carpentaria. Fringed by she-oaks

DOI: 10.4324/9780429328657-8

and surrounded by an abundance of fish and shellfish, Mornington is the traditional home of the Lardil people. The island was not occupied by white missionaries until 1914, after which many other peoples from the mainland were sent there. Old Doomadagee, located on the traditional lands of the Waanyi and Gangalidda people, was set up as a mission in 1933, on the coast; it was moved inland following a cyclone to a site on the Nicholson River. There has been considerable movement between the two communities: in the early part of the last century, people fled to Mornington to get away from the more restrictive rules imposed by missionaries at Doomadgee. Their shared history is embedded in the genocide and dispossession of Aboriginal and Torres Strait Islander peoples, and most people have a connection to the Stolen Generation and to the punitive "welfare" policies imposed by missionaries as arms of the State. Punitive policies continue to shape life in both communities:

> Both … have been subject to Alcohol Management Plans, implemented by the Queensland Government since 2003, which restricts alcohol use in Doomadgee and prohibits it on Mornington Island. This initiative was implemented as a means of reducing the incidence of violent crime, child abuse, and neglect associated with alcohol consumption. However, the Crime and Misconduct Commission (2009) observed there has been no reduction in the number of offences since Alcohol Management Plans were introduced and Mornington Island now has one of the highest rates of violence of all Queensland's Indigenous communities due to the rise of illegal *homebrew*.
>
> (Dawes *et al.* 2017: 309)

In 1991, Australia's Human Rights Commission (HREUC, 1991: 1) noted, "the people of Mornington Island live in a social, economic and political situation which would never be acceptable to non-Aboriginal people living in most parts of Australia". Around two decades later, in 2009, Doomadgee and Mornington Island were among 29 remote communities identified as requiring a "concentrated and accelerated approach to tackling deep-seated disadvantage … geared at developing new ways of working … [and] a focus on getting things right" (Aboriginal and Torres Strait Islander Social Justice Commissioner, 2010, cited in Dawes *et al.* 2017: 309).

"Your knowledge and my knowledge together"

Glenn Dawes, an academic at James Cook University Townsville, and Andrea Davidson, who had been working as a psychologist at the Healing Centres, were interviewed for this case study. As non-Indigenous and non-local people, Glenn and Andrea worked with local Indigenous well-being officers Edward (Beau) Walden and Sarah Isaacs as co-researchers on the project. Glenn explained how he came to be involved, as an outsider:

> I was invited onto the project. And before I took part in the project, I met with Sarah and Beau and Andrea in a hotel room in Cairns, and it was really like a vetting process, I think, for them to see if I was okay.

Beau and Sarah had been working at the Healing Centres, and Andrea, having had previous professional contact with Glenn through mutual involvement in youth justice, invited him to be part of the research team and to help apply for the funding. As Glenn described:

> So, right from the start, I didn't profess to know everything, and I didn't profess to have all the answers, but I did say this is a co-production in terms of your knowledge and my knowledge together. And maybe we can get something out of it in terms of the real question, which is about reducing recidivism, really high rates of recidivism.

From the outset, both Glenn and Andrea acknowledged the need to work with the community to undertake the research, and for the community to drive the research, as Andrea observed:

> You have to be fundamentally tied to the principle of self-determination, and that community will decide what the research should be. You can go to them with broad concepts.
>
> (Andrea)

> You have to involve local people because they have the answers most of the time.
>
> (Glenn)

Both Andrea and Glenn expressed a commitment to empowering the community and to social justice principles, as Glenn made clear: *"I've always come from a framework of social justice and fairness for people"*. The commitment to self-determination pervaded the whole project. A foundational principle was the idea that the project was to be about shared knowledge, as Andrea hints:

> We went in with the statistics and gave them, 'This is what we know' … giving them an understanding of the importance of, and that what they're feeling was true.

Statistics on the overrepresentation of Aboriginal and Torres Strait Islander people confirmed what local people already knew: that young men, in particular, were being imprisoned regularly; that reintegration back into the community was often problematic; and that reoffending rates were high. As Glenn explained:

> It was … mapping in terms of hotspots, and it's very easy to see that there are big, hot spots in these remote communities. … There's not a lot of stuff going on around reintegration.

In this process, exemplifying Glenn's "your knowledge and my knowledge together", there was a recognition of the different skills and knowledge brought to the project: by providing statistical information Glenn and Andrea were contributing what they had to offer the community as professional and academic researchers. The expectation of reciprocity was set up at an early stage and continued throughout the project.

"They'll show you where your spot is"

For Andrea, working as a psychologist at the Healing Centres,

> The starting point for me was certainly being … having that 12 months before we even started conceiving of this research project to really embed in community and just go through all of those really important kind of relational approaches to community.

This allowed the building of relationships and allowed the community to see that the team was "sticking around":

> If you're invested in community, and community accepts you, they'll tell you that. And they'll tell you really, really loud and clear … you've got to prove yourself that you're actually worthy to be there and do that. And then when you are, and you prove that, they'll show you where your spot is.

Embedding themselves in the community, seeking to understand and be understood, was seen as a foundational stage in the research, before any formal research can take place:

> Once you are embedded it's a natural cultural vetting process.
>
> (Andrea)

Gaining the knowledge and awareness necessary to properly conduct yourself is emphasised. Being shown "where your spot is" requires a willingness to be guided and educated and an attitude of humility and openness, which Glenn described thus:

> So it's all that stuff around trust and rapport before you pull the microphone out, just start talking to people. You've got to really get that trust in people.

Aboriginal peoples are widely considered to be the most researched people in the world (recall Merata Mita on New Zealand's "history of people putting Maori under a microscope", in Chapter 2). Having seen little benefit from all this research it is hardly surprising that many communities are wary of researchers, as Glenn was clearly aware:

> If you don't go in there with the right intention, ... people can see through it pretty quickly, these people have seen lots of this happen before – fly-in fly-out, so to speak.

Research as a tool of the ongoing colonial project presents an undeniable barrier to genuine trusting and equal relations. Nevertheless, as Andrea explained, through the relationships she had established in the communities, she was able to serve as the guarantor of Glenn's trustworthiness:

> I was going to have to vouch for Glenn and his approach – his goodness, really. Frankly, they've had so many researchers come in and out of the community.

Glenn himself recognised that as a total outsider he needed to work on establishing local contacts:

> These flights [to the communities] were full of white government workers. And I was just another one of them ... so you really had to have those connections in the community.

As a non-Indigenous researcher, Glenn spent considerable time in the communities engaging in consultative processes before the commencement of the research:

> And basically being seen as well in public places is really important, so I used to hang around the bakery ... and just talk to people.

As an outsider, the need to adapt to the norms and culture of the community was key:

> Of course, you don't turn up in a suit. ... And you're willing to put up with a certain amount of shit to some degree, because some

people will test you out fairly early to find out whether you're genuine or not.

(Glenn)

"Learning to shut up and to listen"

Adapting to different styles of relating and researching was seen as an important learning process, adopting different rhythms of listening and communicating:

Learning to shut up and to listen is another really valuable thing ... it (is) different in our culture because people don't really like extended silences.

(Glenn)

Time also needed to be taken to co-produce the questions and approaches to gathering knowledge and for the teams to use their unique skills – Glenn as a professional researcher and Andrea as a clinician and scholar – to formulate what they would put to the co-researchers and then the community. As Andrea reflected:

We needed to put so much lead time in it. There was a lot of time to really think through and research the best approaches ... it forced us ... going and reflecting ... we were going to have to just drop the impatience, ... that was actually a good thing because it did mean that Glenn and I spent a lot of time just chewing the fat and kind of thinking 'we could go this way or that way', or 'what about we put that to them'?

This time taken to develop the methodology, as Glenn affirmed, was critical:

The methodology was so important – we couldn't have got to where we got without it.

Acknowledging the importance of self-determination, by emphasising community control from the outset, committed the researchers to a methodology that recognised the importance of local knowledge and local networks. Glenn alluded to these aspects of co-production:

The whole methodology was co-designed with the community.

Methodology becomes more than a technocratic, project planning process when a commitment to empowerment and local control leads to an iterative approach that honours these principles from the project's inception, as he hinted:

> We had the broad framework when we wrote the proposal ... and those guidelines were there as it was funded by the Federal Government.
>
> (Glenn)

While the constraints of the research grant informed their approach, the approach to sharing knowledge and identifying the focus together – *with* the elders and other community members – from the beginning meant that there was considerable community support for the project. The research team was insistent that the interview questions be co-produced with the community, in a process that Andrea recounted:

> So, what are the questions we should be asking? If the ultimate aim of this project is to keep particularly our young men here and not in prison, and give a better service to the whole community around how we support all of that. What are the questions we ask? What are the questions we ask about this terrible statistic?
>
> ...
>
> And this project was about telling that story. And then it was very clear to us early on ... Glenn, I remember, he was just like, "Yep, they know exactly the questions that we need to ask." And then we had a base level series of the protocol that came from that, and that protocol was very broad ... then Sarah and Beau were really the ones that developed the questions. ... Glenn did the structuring, but it was workshopped particularly hard with them [the Indigenous co-researchers].

This iterative approach to formulating the questions to be asked meant that "workshopping" the details of the methodology became an ongoing process over many months. This took place on a number of different levels: as consultation between Glenn and Andrea, then Glenn and Andrea with Beau and Sarah, and then the research team with the various sectors of the community, as Glenn conveyed:

> So they helped us reframe the questions and that's why the project was organic, because we constantly kind of change through consultation, which is part of the action research methodology. Back and forth, and with the time not being a huge variable.

The researchers emphasised the need to continually reflect on how the project was being conducted, in terms of cultural competence. Giving space for co-production to continue throughout the implementation of the project, rather than just in the planning, meant that the way interviews were conducted and social interactions occurred needed to be in keeping with cultural norms and values.

"Move lightly and gently"

As the project developed, the need for consultation and cultural sensitivity continued to be of paramount importance, as Andrea emphasised:

> As researchers, we had to move lightly and gently, had to spend months, not in one trip but come in and out and be available before we did any research.

The commitment to spend time listening and learning from the community allowed for the development of trust. Moving "lightly and gently" in a way that respects the rhythms of the community takes longer than a more traditional research approach, as Glenn suggested:

> If there's a death, well, you just gotta ride with that, and sorry business[2] may go on for several days. I had a couple of instances where I went to Mornington Island where everything was called off, so I had to wait for the plane for another two days, basically just hanging around and talk[ing] to people.

Remoteness brings pressure on researchers due to the prohibitive cost of travel:

> Okay, you're a bit pissed off personally. You spent all this money to get there. You wanted some results.
>
> (Glenn)

However, cultural competence and sensitivity to the rhythms of the community require a flexible attitude to time. Therefore, the interviews proceeded in a way that responded to the need for flexibility and that allowed the researchers to access community members who may not have come forward initially:

> the interviews, for example, it was very much a snowballing effect. So people found people, and that was part of the trust-building and the rapport-building. ... We had people who we never planned to interview, never knew about.
>
> (Glenn)

The decision to co-produce with the community raises questions about representation, equity, and access. Some groups may be in a better position to respond and be seen as authoritative members of the community, as Glenn articulated:

> Sometimes the initial people you meet are the people in power that might be on the council. 'Oh, you got to talk to these people. These are the most important people for this project.' 'You got to talk to this family over here' I said, 'Fine. Okay, great.' I actually ran into somebody else who belonged to the other clan, the other clan said, 'How come you're only talking to them? How come you're not talking to us?'

In all communities, there are voices that are privileged above others. The need to avoid treating communities as homogenous, thereby further marginalising sectors that may not hold positions of power, was a challenge for the researchers. Despite their best efforts – "we were trying to … elevate previously silenced voices" (Glenn) – they acknowledged that the voices of women were underrepresented in the project.

One of the challenges for co-production in qualitative research projects, especially where target communities are small and the subject matter is sensitive, is the effect of pre-existing relationships on data-gathering, such as through interviews. Closeness to the community can be a disadvantage when the research involves potentially sensitive issues where shame can prevent open discussion. The Indigenous researchers were respected community members and workers at an important local service. The remoteness of the two communities – and their small size – meant that community ties were a double-edged sword when it came to doing qualitative research. While undoubtedly a benefit in relation to the promotion of the project and selection of participants, these factors limited the local researchers' ability to conduct the interviews for the research, as Andrea related:

> There was this beautiful, lovely thing where we'd set this all up, training and protocols and they said 'Nup, we're not doing this, we've spoken to the community.'

The way most non-Indigenous research teams operate would be to reverse this and have the academic researchers develop the research methods and questions, while the local researchers (usually classified as research assistants) carry out the tasks requiring interpersonal communication. The assumption that participants would be more comfortable disclosing personal issues to a member of their own community was indeed embedded in the researchers' initial plans for this project:

> Alongside (the research) ... we established ... a support case-management kind of framework
> ... the young men in community that were in those facilities, made connections with those facilities.

The need to demonstrate that the researchers were invested in the community, were not fly-in fly-out ("FIFO") workers but people committed to really identifying and responding to the needs of local people, was crucial for the success of the project, as Glenn made clear:

> So the community needed to see us doing that ... and we did it as part of the consultations. They needed to see that before everyone back in community was willing to really get invested.

The remoteness of the two communities added another dimension to the difficulties caused by the high rates of imprisonment, as prisons and juvenile detention centres are located over a thousand kilometres away in the northern Queensland cities of Cairns, Townsville, and Rockhampton. Dedicated flights were used to transport people to and from these centres. These flights had a nickname:

> Con Air, they call it. You know what I mean?
>
> (Glenn)

This efficient removal to prison contrasts sharply with the lack of attention paid to getting people back to their community. Many people recently released from prison are rearrested on their way home, the lack of post-release support to make the 1,000-kilometre journey leading to some being stranded in urban centres like Cairns.

In response to this pressing and immediately resolvable issue, one detention centre was able to provide audiovisual link (AVL) facilities for families to speak to loved ones in prison, which had a huge positive impact on the ability of the team to research in the way they ultimately did, as Andrea explained:

> And then when we were doing things like going, 'Hey, let's fix things here. Let's set it up so video conferences can be run every week.' 'We can run a visit schedule. Let's set it up so that we bring some elders down. Let's set it up so that we know when you're coming home.'

And so we got some like outcomes before we actually even started the formal research part of it.

The way that the project findings were reported back to the community became an integral part of the project and further demonstrated community ownership of the project:

> Community said, 'you know, at the end of all this, we, we don't want some big fat report that we're never gonna read. And, you know, he's going to sit up in the library. We want you to come back and tell us, and we want you to make a video about it.' That's how we gave it back to Community.
>
> (Andrea)

A collection of videos[3] that reported on the results was made in addition to the regular meetings with community, and these involved many of the community:

> All of the actors in that were staff, either staff at the Wellbeing centre, or people we'd engaged as we were helping them to transition out of prison, lots of different people got involved with that.
>
> (Andrea)

The involvement of the project participants in telling the story of the research findings can be seen as another layer in the co-productive fabric of the research. As Glenn explained:

> We used local actors to make six small films around some of the issues that came out of the report, for educational purposes.

"Back off and put your pen away"

The Keeping on Country documentary[4] represents one aspect of the enduring effect of the research. In terms of other outcomes, the final report highlighted the need for community-based responses to "the problem of recidivism" (Dawes, 2016) and recommended a justice reinvestment approach:

> Aboriginal people in each community have clear ideas about what could work in their communities. These ideas to reduce recidivism have been clearly articulated from grassroots local people, who know what the problems are and have pragmatic solutions to these problems. Justice Reinvestment is the catalyst to make these solutions a reality,

creating a break in this geographical disadvantage by providing funds to create capacity for alternative pathways for dealing with the recidivist problem.

(Dawes, 2016: 100)

While this suggestion was not picked up by the Federal or State government, the communities' overwhelming support for "on country" camps has been acknowledged and pilot projects[5] initiated. Two other elements of the project – the case management initiative providing support for people released from prison, and the audiovisual links to connect people in prison with the community – have continued.

Considerable structural barriers exist to the co-production of research in remote communities, as Glenn reflected:

When the university people say, 'Hey look, the project is about to run out. You've done the two years.' You've got to come back and say, "Hey, you need to understand that we need longer than two years. We're not quite there yet. So just back off and put your pen away, and this might go on for another year."

The Keeping on Country example suggests that a general non-Indigenous research model is inappropriate, at least for remote Aboriginal and Torres Strait Islander communities. Practices like independently formulating the research question and methodology, or scheduling fieldwork without reference to the people being researched, reproduce colonising processes and entrench colonial relations. As Andrea warns:

You can't just go in and say 'we're going to show up on Tuesday' … there's a whole range of engagements around saying 'should we do this, how should this be done, who should it be done with and what should be done with it.'

However, the researchers emphasised the need to work with individual communities to develop specific terms and practices; a one-size-fits-all approach is never appropriate. While the overall impact of the research initially appeared small, in terms of policy change, the highly political and reactive nature of criminal justice made it unpredictable:

Well, strangely enough, this is since I've spoken to you, the Queensland government have … everyone's read my report, and lots of politicians have actually said to me, 'This "on country" idea is a really good idea.'

(Glenn)

In any case, the Keeping on Country project shows it is possible to co-produce research in an ethical, culturally sensitive way that accommodates funding and academic constraints, but that still places the concerns of affected communities at the centre of the work.

Notes

1 Maggie was not able to visit Far North Queensland to interview the two other researchers or any of the community partners. We acknowledge this is a limitation. Only interviewing two non-Indigenous researchers – and none of the Aboriginal participants – means that we present a partial perspective on this project. That is not to discount the researchers' reflections as authentic and genuinely conveying their insights into how the project was initiated and how it unfolded. But we acknowledge that other participants, particularly those living in Community, on Country, would have different points of view.
2 Sorry business refers to the rituals observed during a period of mourning.
3 Available on the North West Remote Health website: https://www.nwrh.com.au/who-are-we/projects/
4 Available on the North West Remote Health website: https://www.nwrh.com.au/who-are-we/projects/ and via YouTube: https://www.youtube.com/watch?v=mixEf-kTZD8
5 For examples, see: https://campingoncountry.com.au/; or Mona Aboriginal Corporation's 'On Country' program in Mount Isa, Queensland. https://www.abc.net.au/news/2020-11-18/indigenous-on-country-program-helping-mount-isa-youth/12886356

References

Dawes, G (2016) *Keeping on country: Doomadgee and Mornington Island recidivism research report*. Townsville: North and West Remote Health.
Dawes, G, Davidson, A, Walden, E & Isaacs, S (2017) Keeping on country: Understanding and responding to crime and recidivism in remote Indigenous communities, *Australian Psychologist*, 52(4): 306–315.
HREOC, Human Rights and Equal Opportunity Commission (1991) *Mornington: A report by the Federal Race Discrimination Commissioner* Canberra: Commonwealth of Australia.

Part 3

7 The *whats* and *what-ifs* of co-production

In Part I, the opening two chapters, we examined concepts of co-production and their application in criminal justice, then explored some of the theoretical undercurrents we identified as shaping the Justice context. In Part II, we used case studies to delve into particular examples of what people *do* when they co-produce knowledge in/about criminal justice, to understand their motivations and capture the complexities they encounter in practice. Now in Part III, across Chapters 7 and 8, we draw out the tensions, paradoxes, and possibilities that co-production holds and reveals in the criminal justice context. We return to the questions we started with at the beginning of this book: What or who makes the "co" in co-production? What or who makes co-production in and about criminal justice distinct from co-production in other contexts?

From our thematic coding and analysis of the case studies, we drew a set of themes that are useful for exploring these and other questions that arose. Figure 7.1 shows how these themes emerged through our analysis (see Appendix 1 for details). These themes coalesced under the rubrics of *time*, *space*, and *identity*. We see these themes operating as technologies of power, encompassing both micro and macro dimensions, which we explore in this chapter. We think about these intersecting themes through the lens of power (and the diffuse and relational ways in which power operates) and hierarchy (or structures of domination and relations of superiority), and ways of knowing (in terms of the power to define, to construct people's identity, to commodify stories of adversity or redemption), which are concepts that we developed in Chapter 2. These are important threads we pick up now, in this chapter, and weave through our analysis.

In analysing the case studies, we are *thinking with* these ideas – to consider the straightforward ways they appear in and across the different examples, and to explore deeper layers of meaning that they open up or illustrate. Each theme, therefore, is presented as follows: we start with the familiar, readily apparent ways each theme manifests in criminal justice settings; we

DOI: 10.4324/9780429328657-10

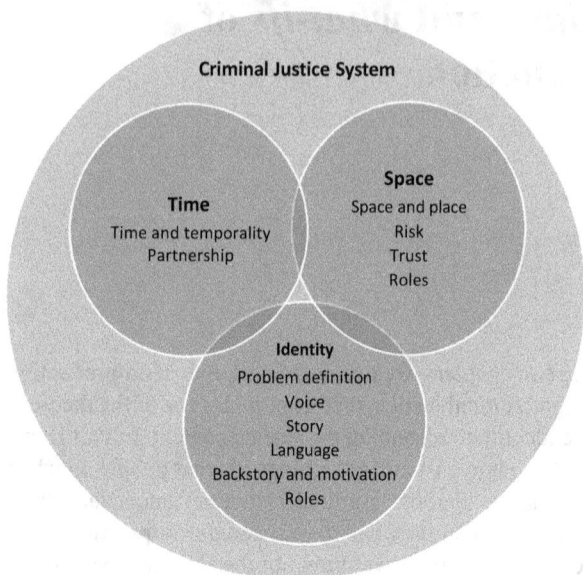

Figure 7.1 Themes emerging from the theory-oriented qualitative analysis of the case studies

then identify and elaborate several sub-themes before concluding with the *what-ifs* – the potential and possibilities that co-production holds.

Time

Time is a familiar theme in the criminal justice milieu, a thread running through prison tropes and courtroom vernacular. Punishment, for example, is "calibrated in chunks of time" (Liebling & Maruna, 2005: 3): a term of imprisonment, a prison sentence, a life sentence, a suspended sentence, a non-parole period, time served, bail, remand, parole, probation, court orders. All are associated with a period, a length of time. Prison, similarly, is marked by temporality: serving time, hard time, wasted time, "dead time", "empty time", "lost time" (Medlicott, 1999; Guenther, 2013). The idea of "doing time" is embedded in adages such as *do the crime, do the time*, and *do the time, don't let the time do you*. The ceaseless repetition and waiting that characterises prison temporality – the "urgent demand to do nothing – to hurry up and wait" – attests to carceral power over time (Guenther, 2013: 196). Even post-release, the "offender" is "condemned to be left hanging"

(McNeill, 2019: 2) – waiting for appointments, in parole offices, in welfare queues – waiting in/on/for someone else's time.

The case studies feature many familiar temporal elements. Chapter 3's User Voice example illustrates the mundane yet profound structuring effects of prison lockdown on people's existence, including their movements and everyday activities. The Youth Justice case study in Chapter 5 shows young people using their participation in a research project as a way of "killing time", dealing with the boredom of confinement. We also discern subtle yet specific ways these temporal themes seem to run through the case studies, which suggests they are particular to and/or associated with co-production in the justice milieu. These are the temporal "whats" of co-production that emerge from the case studies: *linear time*; *bureaucratic time*; and *being ready*. We follow these themes with a brief consideration of the *what if*, that is, the possibility of how justice-imposed time might be challenged, interrupted, rescheduled, even "re-tempoed" by co-production and its demands.

Linear time

The prevailing Western way in which time is conceived, understood, and experienced is in linear, chronological terms. Co-production time is defined by project time, time frames, timelines, all of which have a clear beginning, middle, and end. This is "official time". Through this lens, time is segmented, boxed, and limited. Three examples from our case studies are illustrative: both the Youth Justice example and the Mothers Project were conceived as three-year PhD projects – according to university requirements – yet the latter, in particular, was built on years of preparation and follow up; Keeping on Country was similarly shaped by Commonwealth government funding timelines and university constraints. Time in these contexts is structured and approved by outside entities. It is determined elsewhere.

Externally defined project time frames dictate project spending: how much money is spent, and when, and how much time is spent building relationships. Yet this often means the time before and after a project – within which human relationships develop and flourish – is disappeared, hidden, rendered invisible. We could conceive this time as "moving at the speed of trust" (Brown, 2017), which of course runs counter to project timelines. The invisible relational work, the time it takes to build relationships, and its ongoing investment does not feature on budget spreadsheets. These "costs" are carried by individuals and communities who invest in relationships over time – and this is the time that is unrecognised and unaccounted for. Labours of love are elided as "in-kind" contributions or not mentioned at all. Who does this work, we wonder? And what does it mean to work relationally, at the speed of trust, within linear project time?

The time–cost relationship is articulated in the Mothers' Project. Sinead describes seeking funding for her research, to cover "the actual financial costs":

> Had I not fought for that funding, fought and applied for that funding it wouldn't have been possible ... there would be no Mothers' Project, as much as they want participatory work and a participatory study.

Importantly, concerning time, Sinead points out:

> [The costs] didn't end for me when the project ended although it did for the university.

Here she is referring to the financial costs as well as the time invested: a project funded for three years that took place over more than eight years and continues. Similarly, Straight Talking relied on years of preparatory, collaborative work that began two decades earlier. The State's financial investment in such a project is contingent upon the time and work of individuals and communities already having been done. Projects and the time allocated appear to be based on an unstated understanding of an investment (of time, energy, relational work), before and after the time allotted (i.e. funded). Project time, then, is always limited in linear terms, yet often relies on more circular notions of time as organic, fluid, flowing, and ongoing. These different temporal registers and relations to time remind us that co-production is about relationships and trust, and that time conceived in linear limited terms is inimical to the flourishing of these human elements, themes we pick up further below.

Bureaucratic time

Bureaucratic time runs to its own uneven rhythm. It slows – drags, stalls – and it speeds up, demanding urgent responses. Perhaps, as Habdankaitė (2017) argues, *delay* – this repetitive waiting and stalling – both characterises and constitutes bureaucratic power, the coordination of which rests on a "disjointed and delayed temporality" (p.71-2). We can observe some of the finer contours of this paradox in the case of Keeping on Country. The (non-Indigenous) co-researchers highlight different conceptions of time that we describe in terms of *clock time*, which is linear, "calendrical and scheduled" (Iparraguirre, 2015: 623), and *event time*, which is more elastic and based on cycles, seasons, social obligations, and rituals. The rhythms of life in the

Mornington Island and Doomadgee communities highlight the rigidity of the project's bureaucratic time frames and show the coexistence of these different temporalities.

Keeping on Country reveals long histories and relationships built over extended periods. Trying to impose 9 to 5 "city time" over local time – by constructing Keeping on Country as a project with a beginning, middle, and end – did not correspond to the "tempos of ordinary life" in community (Rifkin, 2017). When there is a death in the community, for example, rather than fitting a preordained period of bereavement leave, "sorry business may go on for several days" and involve time spent "hanging around and talking to people" (Glenn). Other rhythms of daily life, including "lying around in the morning", render city time meaningless. Similarly, for the (non-Indigenous) researchers, as outsiders, the importance of gradual familiarity and of "being seen in public places" meant it was "important ... to hang around the bakery ... and just talk to people" (Glenn). Whereas from a bureaucratic perspective "hanging around" may be perceived as time wasted, from a co-production perspective, this time is crucial to give space for relationships, trust, and familiarity to start to grow.

The remoteness of the community – far away from big cities and densely populated areas – has temporal as well as spatial implications. It takes a long time to get to and from other places. When people are transported on dedicated flights (locally known as "Con Air") to prisons over a thousand kilometres away, and then released without resources to get home, they can often become stranded in between. This example shows how the jagged rhythm of settler colonial "justice time" – the rush of intake, the abrupt discharge – contrasts sharply with people's slow drift back to Country. In this way, "hegemonic temporality" (Iparraguirre 2015) dominates and disrupts the rhythms of life for the local Lardil, Waanyi, and Gangalidda people, as it does in the lives of Indigenous peoples everywhere. As Rifkin (2017: xiii) points out, though, there are "possibilities for self-determination and Indigenous duration that arise in being out of sync with settler time". The Keeping on Country project – being on Country – needed to adopt a different tempo to attune to the "cultural rhythmics"[1] (Iparraguirre, 2015) of the community.

Thus, for settler occupiers on Aboriginal land, co-producing with First Nations peoples requires temporal shifts, shedding fixed ideas and time frames, and letting go of power and authority (see, for example, Bawaka Country, 2015[2]). Iparraguirre (2015: 623) (working with Indigenous societies in Argentina's Chaco region) usefully distinguishes different yet coexisting temporalities: hegemonic temporality is routine and linear, and reflects a "projective attitude", while Indigenous rhythms pay attention to *what is to come*. For the Keeping on Country researchers, different temporal conceptions required an "organic" process of going "back and forth" with "time not being a huge variable" (Glenn); "we had to move lightly and gently, had to spend months, not in one trip but come in and out and be available before we did any research" (Andrea). In this way, though the project was framed in Justice terms, the paradox is that bureaucratic time was necessarily subsumed by local time.

The Birds Eye View podcast shows another example of different concepts of and relations to time, moving at the speed of trust and relationships, and the parallels and discordance with prison time. The clash of time frames was evident in the way the imprisoned women's storytelling was initially conceived as an "event" – a once-off, short-term solution that imposed a temporality that would interrupt (a much smaller group of) listeners' time only momentarily, a fleeting interaction that may have little purchase in any collective memory. Yet the way the Birds Eye View project developed, as the women of the Darwin Correctional Centre and their allies became involved and the relationships between them started to shape its direction, the time frames stretched and lengthened. The podcast became an enduring temporal artefact, something that lives on, well beyond the life of the project itself. It now exists as a permanent record of 12 women's individual personal stories, a series of ten beautifully produced, yet raw and authentic audio recordings, with subsequent episodes promising an ongoing conversation.

Birds Eye View has thus surpassed its original aim to reveal "What's it like to be a woman in a man's prison?" It represents a push back against the paradox of bureaucratic time that both slows and suspends the lives of people imprisoned while punctuating those lives with its outward managerial focus on efficiency, outputs, and measures of effectiveness. The project indeed provides a bird's eye view of prison life, the minutiae of its daily rhythms and frustrations, in ways that challenge quantified "tick box" notions of risk and rehabilitation and reframe what it means to "do time" as a woman in a man's prison.

The clash of temporalities, between relational time moving at the speed of trust and bureaucratic time moving according to a range of managerial priorities, is obvious at one level. Yet, at a deeper level, the paradox of bureaucratic time has implications for human relationships that work against the very idea of "doing justice". The bureaucratic segmentation of time that valorises "getting it done on time", for instance, cuts off the continuous nature of the relationships required for the project to happen in the first place. As Tubex (2015) observes, managerialist priorities become problematic – indeed harmful – when they eclipse underlying human needs and broader justice aims such as individuals' accountability to each other, relational healing, and reconnection to community. The examples above show the jaggedness of bureaucratic time, its demands and delays, like a stuttering machine, and how it contrasts with the smooth, slow flow of human time, moving with the seasons and the diurnal rhythms of people and places, ready when they are ready.

Being ready

The notion of readiness is suffused with temporality. In Straight Talking, for instance, mentors are required to have exhausted their parole and not have any compulsory appointments to attend, to be a mentor. Time needs to have elapsed between their own lived experience of criminal justice entanglement and the point at which they can start putting it to use in the service of others. Who knows how long that might take? While this speaks to individuals' rehabilitative preparedness, the concept of readiness has other temporal connotations. Systemic readiness might describe organisations and institutions being ready to adopt co-production principles and practices or to be willing to share power. Cultural and political readiness might refer to moments in history, and broader appetites for thinking and doing things differently, such as the global #BlackLivesMatter movements and COVID-19 have precipitated. Local and national political readiness (and perceptions of political risk) are more often shaped by the current point in the electoral cycle, whether we are "in an election year", for instance. All these kinds of readiness are discernible in the case studies and are arguably at play in the proliferation of co-production activities more widely.

The Keeping on Country project, for example, was commissioned as part of the Federal Government's "Breaking the Cycle" initiative and was specifically focused on reducing incarceration rates (Dawes 2016). Equally, for the Indigenous communities, the problem of people being locked up far away and returning to community, "out of sync" and disconnected, demanded a response. The project exemplified co-production in two ways: it co-produced an intervention, in the form of audiovisual links that enabled family video conferencing visits to maintain connection to community during periods of incarceration, and it co-produced knowledge about the context of the intervention, through the research. This approach was unprecedented: "To this point there were no other studies which attempted to gain the perceptions of Indigenous people about the problem of recidivism and its impacts on remote communities" (Dawes, 2016: iii). This suggests a degree of readiness on the part of government decision-makers to fund and support methods that embody self-determination, for which First Nations people have been calling for generations (though whether any real change has resulted from the project is yet to be seen).

Further, the Keeping on Country project produced a range of artefacts, including the 140-page report (Dawes, 2016) and academic articles (Dawes *et al.* 2017; Dawes & Davidson, 2019). But it also yielded videos and resources that were produced with and by the community, for the community. This also signalled readiness on the part of academics and universities to orient their research practices around the people they are researching, to think about "knowledge" (and "evidence") differently, and to partner with communities in meaningful ways. Though framed in and on Justice terms, Keeping on Country illustrates how a co-production project had to adopt a different tempo, to attune to the "cultural rhythmics" (Iparraguirre, 2015) of the community, and its needs and priorities. In this way co-production on Country demanded the "re-tempoing" of Justice rhythms. And Justice seemed ready to follow.

What if

Here, as indicated earlier, we explore the possibility of how justice-imposed time might be challenged, interrupted, rescheduled, and even "re-tempoed" by co-production and its demands. We have used the examples of Keeping on Country and Birds Eye View to illustrate some of the ways that co-production pushes back against linear time – how it demands the cultural rhythmics of "give and take". We've explored how this demand for flexibility and mutuality can stretch the punctuation marks of "justice time", rendering its syntax and grammar paradoxically more legible and illegible, more relevant and irrelevant, at the same time. We've shown that, in holding different temporalities together, co-production can thus offer a means of shifting power relations, albeit subtly and slowly, and how this capacity to thereby interrupt "justice time" holds promise and opportunities for working–making–doing differently. We've also seen, however, that change requires readiness. Being ready takes time, relational time that moves at the speed of trust. And trust cannot be hurried.

Justice pervades people's lives temporally and spatially (McNeill, 2019). Just as prison is a "time-place" (Medlicott, 1999), so too is the landscape of justice in the community, where correctional supervision, psychological treatment, and other mandated support services comprise a web of temporal and spatial control over people's lives and everyday routines. For example, both service providers and their "clients" are regulated by the way programmes are delivered: contracts, budgets, eligibility criteria, and performance indicators dictate these parameters. "Success" is measured according to predetermined outcomes, and "clients" are responsibilised for their rehabilitation. Such is the landscape of the managerialist, technocratic criminal justice described in Chapter 1 (and explained further in Chapter 2). We also noted, however, that practitioners often operate within this cultural, political, economic context with a certain ambivalence, bringing to bear overriding principles and ethical motivations in their work with communities.

Such creative approaches, in signalling workers' inclination to work *with* their clients, could create the conditions for co-production relationships to flourish by making room for resistance against managerialist and bureaucratic constraints. If we think about co-*production* as inherently oriented to creation and creativity – to making or producing things – this seems to make sense. Earlier we mentioned how people can be "condemned to be left hanging" (McNeill, 2019: 2) – waiting in queues, for appointments, for transport home – and how waiting and delay characterise bureaucratic power over time and people's lives. We have seen that waiting can also be the undoing of this power, a site of resistance and "re-tempoing" of the justice machinery to human scales of movement through time and space. This can occur on the part of "service users" and service providers, both of whom can be seen as constrained, albeit unequally and in different ways, by bureaucratic time and its demands. What if, through co-production, the grip of the justice system over people's lives might be loosened, its tempo adjusted to human relational time? What if, in this way, co-producing means creating space for this to arise?

Space

Criminal justice settings comprise a range of places and spaces: inside and outside, concrete and symbolic. These include closed spaces that are physically, psychologically, or affectively bounded; in-between, liminal spaces that are "neither here nor there" (Johns, 2018); and social spaces structured by the kind of power relations we explored in Chapter 2. Safety, security, and access restrictions infuse all of these. Questions of worker safety in criminal justice settings often centre on spatial considerations: the locations of egress points, for example, or the physical positioning of furniture. Other questions of safety hinge on perceived risks to "clients" (on the part of workers) such as the contamination of younger children through proximity to more experienced teenagers in youth justice. How justice spaces *feel* is part of how they are experienced, too, of course. For instance, in Chapter 5, Tim observed that, for young people, youth detention felt risky and unsafe when workers were "less engaged and lackadaisical and don't take that adult, leadership role", as "the "effective parent" on the unit"; that, for young people in secure settings, where the risk of violence may be imminent, "it's about authority and safety. Authority that says, "I'm here to help and keep you safe and maintain the rules; I'm here to help maintain order'"". From this perspective, maintaining "the rules" and "order" in a place shapes the safety and security of spaces in both material and psychological ways.

Space and place thus encompass *where* we are and *who* we are in terms of our embodied sense of self and in relation to others and the world around us (which thus connects with identity, explored further below). Spatiality and temporality are entwined; both comprise a set of relations. The spaces, settings, and sites of criminal justice can be delineated through the relations used to describe it: as something imposed on, administered by, experienced as, delivered to, on behalf of, achieved through, fought for, or brought about; having jurisdiction over, being under an order. All these terms indicate directional, temporal, spatial (and power) relationships between individuals, populations, institutions, and processes. There is something else about criminal justice spaces, however, in that they are both seen and unseen, known and unknown; within ken and yet removed. We are often spectators but rarely witnesses to these spaces (Brown, 2009). In this way, we observe a paradox between the close restrictiveness of prison spaces – the lack of natural light, limited airflow, and forced proximity between bodies in shared cells – and the distance (physical, legal, moral, social, emotional) between prison and the community: a paradox of proximity.

As many have observed (e.g. Foucault, 1977; Davis, 2003), the function of the prison is to erase the spectacle of punishment. Hidden from view and surrounded by impenetrable walls, often in remote locations, contemporary prisons supposedly transform punishment from pre-modern visceral forms of public execution into sanitised, unseen penal practices carried out in out-of-the-way places. Yet popular imagery of crime and criminals, prisons and prisoners, conveyed and perpetuated through media narratives, othering tropes and stereotypes, give the impression that criminal justice places and spaces are known and familiar. The spectacle of punishment is magnified in many ways through these new media. We "know" what the inside of an execution chamber looks like, we are familiar with the sound of jangling keys and clanging steel doors on a televised prison wing, or the rap of a judge's gavel. These sensory and spatial images carried in our minds and evoked through everyday sights and sounds – such as the flashing lights and sirens of police cars – shape our ideas about things of which most of us have no direct experience. Thus, as Angela Davis (2003: 15) writes, "the prison is present in our lives and, at the same time, it is absent from our lives".

This raises the issue of proximity both as a spatial dimension and its implications in terms of "penal spectatorship" (Brown, 2009), which relies on distance between a culturally constructed "us" and "them" (the criminalised other). This distance allows us to see the criminalised other as different from us, a lesser human – or even less than human – and highlights how proximity can function to close this distance, to challenge the "spectator" to become "witness" to another's humanity (Brown, 2009). A self-described returning citizen captures this in a tweet reflecting on their exchange with a politician:

> Rep – Do you think ppl who committed murder should be released?
> Me – Absolutely. I committed a murder. (Explained story)
> After our conversation
> Rep – you're the first person to commit murder I have met!!
>
> This is why EVERY politician should visit a prison. All about Proximity.
> (@DavidEGarlock, Twitter, May 22, 2021)

This example illustrates the way everyday assumptions about crime and criminalised people are politicised through distance but can also be dispelled through human interactions that bring us into proximity, a theme we delve into further below.

Beyond these broader social-relational aspects, the case studies reveal many spatial elements, often appearing in obvious yet unexpected ways: the highly regulated and controlled maximum-security prison spaces to which User Voice was granted access, including "on the wing"[3], and the relatively open areas of the prison in which the Prison Council meetings were held, for instance (Chapter 3). Beyond these more conspicuous examples, space – in material and symbolic forms – was more subtly inhabited and navigated in various ways across the case examples. We articulate these – the spatial "whats" of co-production in criminal justice settings – under the headings: *access*, *proximity*, and *risk, and safety*. We explain, below, how each of these themes manifests in the case studies, and then turn to consider the *what-ifs* – the possibilities for justice spaces to be reconfigured, reinhabited, or experienced differently through co-production and its demands.

Access

The ability to get in and get out of places – who can come and go, and who must negotiate access, such as through permissions and human research ethics approval processes – is one aspect determining how space and place are experienced. These elements of the case studies reflect how power is wielded, exchanged, used, gained, and lost through the performance of different roles and identities (as we explore further below). The most obvious example is that of access to the prison: who is there under coercion (compulsorily) and who can enter and exit freely; Garry (of User Voice) having the keys to most of the prison was striking given his extensive history of criminalisation and imprisonment (Chapter 3). This access relied on the official and governmental trust invested in User Voice as an organisation, which then authorised each of its employees to act on its behalf and carry out its work, while at the same time demonstrating their individual story of redemption and reform; this, in turn, sustained that trust. Spatial access is thus shown to be entwined with moral, legal, and social access: each form of certification is contingent upon and productive of the other.

Having access to the "right" people (an example of social access) or the institutional support to make a co-production project "work" relies on certain kinds of power dynamics. Past projects had enabled the women in the Mothers' Project and Birds Eye View – and Tim through his professional experience – to demonstrate their worthiness and trustworthiness, which provided the foundational access for their current projects. In the Mothers' Project, for instance, Sinead was "gifted power" in the form of the keys to the prison, enabling her to "work freely and walk freely between different sections of the prison", a "gift" commented on by one of the imprisoned women: "Jesus, Sinead, look how things have turned around for you, holding those keys". As this remark highlights, movement around the prison is a privilege. In Birds Eye View, for example, once the women became technologically skilled, they would "go out in [the] yard and record", which afforded them a degree of personal agency and freedom not often available in prison (Chapter 4). Establishing relationships with staff was also key, as Johanna explained, describing how Birds Eye View built on the "lineage there of working with artists inside the prison system", specifically the successful *Prison Songs* programme. Similarly, Sinead credits the relationship she established with a prison general manager in her earlier postgraduate study as instrumental in facilitating access for the Mothers' Project.

The case studies illustrate how those holding power, through their existing relationships and access arrangements, could act as proxies for those who did not. For formerly imprisoned men, in Straight Talking, trying to get "back *into* the prison" relied on Claire negotiating access on their behalf, highlighting the power of administrative controls over who comes and goes from the prison, and recalling how delay – and waiting – characterises and constitutes this bureaucratic power. Once they were allowed to re-enter the prison, with official authorisation, Claire noted "the positive spin-off" in that "we have other staff hovering, going, 'Hey can we have them come to my group?'" This revealed another facet of former prisoners' access back into the prison: it represented an opportunity for them to demonstrate their trustworthiness and the extent of their transformation or "rehabilitation". In this way, once more, physical access is emblematic of other social pathways and routes towards acceptability, which connects with the theme of identity, below.

Paradoxically, User Voice had perhaps the most liberal attitude to access, allowing ex-prisoners unfettered access by holding the keys to the prison (literally) because they are contracted (that is, paid by the state) to carry out the work of the prison council. Perhaps this reflects an acknowledgement of the power dynamics within the "society of captives" (Sykes, 1958), within which prison authority is always finely balanced upon the power relations among prisoner social hierarchies; "custodians are engaged in a continuous struggle to maintain order" (Sykes, 1958: 42). User Voice claims that "only offenders can stop reoffending", thereby highlighting the important role of peer workers as allies of both "the ruled" and "the rulers" (Sykes, 1958: 58), the keepers and the confined. The access afforded to User Voice is powerful in both material and symbolic ways. Garry's trustworthiness and thus his certification as an "*ex*-offender" was signified by the power he had to unlock prison doors (Chapter 3). On the other hand, in some community-based projects access was very much determined by considerations of risk, framed in terms of eligibility, whereby "risky populations" like sex offenders were excluded from participating, such as in Straight Talking (Chapter 5). In this way, the long arm of criminal justice is seen to shape access to social acceptability for the criminalised in profound and lasting ways.

The power to grant access to co-production spaces is not always aligned with ultimate power over a project, however, as our Keeping on Country case study reveals (Chapter 6). In parts of Australia, permit laws give Aboriginal people the right to grant or refuse access to their land. People seeking to research on Mornington Island, for example, must have authorisation from the local council. Even with permission granted, the Keeping on Country researchers were clear that their occupation of the space was contingent upon the prior relationships they had established. Keenly aware of the history of "fly in fly out" ("FIFO") researchers in remote communities, they were determined to demonstrate their understanding of the importance of cultural safety, trust, and respect. This meant an emphasis on simply being in the place, just "hanging round", allowing trust to develop slowly. In this way, the local communities exercised a significant degree of power within the project, in terms of sovereignty over their land and waters, and the local temporalities and cultural rhythms discussed above (under "Time"). Yet in other, perhaps more outward-facing ways, the project was still shaped by colonial logics and power structures: the funding arrangements and time frames; the way the problem of men and women being taken from their Country, under legal orders, imprisoned far away, then left to make their own way home, was defined as one of "recidivism".

Ultimately, the title of the project, *Keeping on Country*, signals the fundamental importance of the physical, symbolic, and relational spaces of co-production in developing a genuine understanding of the community and the problems it faces. Keeping on Country means working together, in partnership, with mutual respect and trust providing the conditions whereby access to these spaces might be granted. In this way, co-production might be seen as a method for creating "meeting-points", a means "to foster proximity, creating space for new forms of relational engagement" (Balint *et al.* 2020: 5) that might be sustained beyond the life of a project.

Proximity

Proximity – to people, places, and institutional processes – takes different forms: physical closeness and relational proximity; geographic remoteness; social, emotional, and symbolic distance; and through technologies that mediate "geographies of proximity and distance" (Ó Tuathail, 1996). Beyond these, paradoxical aspects of spatial proximity emerge in the case studies. In prison spaces, for example, privacy is compromised and the idea of the panopticon, pervasive and all-seeing, is reflected in the fishbowl nature of some criminal justice places: observation cells, visiting areas, communal showers, for instance. Yet other spaces are out of sight, closed, inaccessible. In Birds Eye View, the women found private space in the prison library where they could work in proximity to each other and feel safe being together. In the Youth Justice setting, the young men sought to escape the proximity of lockdown by participating in the research interviews.

Proximity as physical closeness means *going to* people or, in the case of Keeping on Country, *going to* Community. In the communities of Far North Queensland, the geographic remoteness is underlined by the fact that flights into the communities "were full of white government workers" (Glenn), while flights out were more often populated by people going to prison, via "Con Air". This geography of distance is mediated, however, through other forms of technology apart from aeroplanes. Audiovisual links enabled proximity between community members and their loved ones in prison, bringing families into the process of people's return from custody, potentially enabling a swifter return home than the usual drift back. Being in proximity can thus mean opening emotional and psychological space, as well as shrinking physical distance. This paradox has become all too familiar since 2020, under conditions of the global pandemic, with digital technologies often the only means of bridging corporeal separation.

As well as the material and digital spaces of co-production, the case studies suggest that a different type of proximity is required in co-production: *bearing witness* to the experience of punishment or desistance (Anderson, 2016), a closeness that involves drawing near and listening. Listening, as Dufourmantelle (2018: 83) observes, "is not one and the other who are listening to each other; it is actually listening that is unfolding between them", implying connection, presence, and proximity. For Tim, listening to the young men's narratives and making sense of these together meant checking with them: "Am I hearing you right? Is this what you're saying?". Being in proximity, in a symbolic sense, also means meeting people where they are – socially, emotionally, temporally – to be able, as Tim described, to "provide them the space to give their narrative" (Chapter 5). Through listening as "the gentlest expression ... of encounter" (Dufourmantelle, 2018: 83), co-producers can meet each other as humans, "giving space" (p.69) for that encounter, and for change to unfold.

Working with people in criminal justice settings and listening to people's stories of trauma, violence, and adversity can take an emotional toll and potentially lead to "burnout", as suggested both in Birds Eye View and by Sinead in the Mothers' Project. The exhaustion and isolation of burnout can also be a manifestation of secondary or vicarious trauma as a result of engaging empathically with the traumatic experiences of others (Collins & Long, 2003). As with any trauma, to heal, "[w]e must sew another skin over the burn left by the event. Create a protective covering" (Dufourmantelle, 2018: 85). Healing demands creation, reconstruction. Dufourmantelle (2018) invokes the sabotage of safety, the destruction and undermining of the self that trauma brings about and observes that "nothing can sew up such a wound. Nothing except creation, what reopens the wound elsewhere and differently, but on less shifting ground" (p.86). Perhaps women coming together "with their backpack of trauma" (Sinead), making space for each other to "feel a sense of community, feel a sense of togetherness and a sense of belonging" (Fiona) – allowing listening to unfold between them, bearing witness to each other's pain – allowed them "to move forward together" (Johanna). Perhaps the spaces for listening created in the three women's projects could "reopen wounds elsewhere and differently ... on less shifting ground" than the women had previously experienced.

In this way, rather than any commodification of pain (a charge frequently levelled at criminal justice researchers and social scientists, as we considered in Chapter 2), the co-production examples we gathered show people in proximity to others' pain – drawing near and listening – without assuming authority over, narrating, or trafficking in their stories. The case studies suggest that genuinely co-producing knowledge – by fostering proximity – can give space for a kind of cognitive justice-making (*cf.* de Sousa Santos, 2014). This proximity to pain carries emotional costs and risks that require safety nets of support and supervision, spaces and places of ongoing safety.

Risk and safety

Risk and safety manifest in the case studies in different ways: the management of risk and security in justice-related workplaces and settings; the importance of emotional and cultural safety and the creation of safe spaces;

political and organisational risks; and the risk of failure or making mistakes. Risk and safety thus have distinct spatial qualities. In correctional settings, safety is usually construed in terms of *risk* – of violence, reoffending, homelessness, and so on. In the case studies, this aspect was certainly present. For women particularly, though, safety pertained to emotional and relational concerns in the immediate and longer term. This was often related to women's traumatic histories and experiences of family violence. Finding space in the highly regulated prison environment of the Mothers' Project, for instance, was critical to allow women to feel safe, to relax, and even to have fun, as Sinead described: "The amount of fun we had ... the laughter ... it was so good". Importantly, as the case studies show, this safe emotional space began with having a safe physical space.

In the Birds Eye View case study, the location in the prison library provided a safe space for the women to work together on the podcast. It was safe in that it offered more privacy than other parts of the prison, it escaped the surveillant gaze of CCTV cameras, and it was quiet. It even allowed the women to use the toilet as an acoustic space for recording vocals. This example highlights the contrast between the co-production space and the rest of the prison where, so often, even the most intimate spaces carry risks of violation, of being watched or assaulted. In the prison setting, which is "not a place where people trust easily" (Johanna), it was important to have a separate area that symbolised some kind of retreat or refuge from the everyday challenges of prison life, including lockdowns or having to "hurry up and wait" (Guenther, 2013) for appointments and compulsory activities. Similarly, for the young people in Youth Justice, being in a space within the prison yet outside of custodial routines afforded them a place to avoid lockdown and – importantly – safe *space to speak* without the concern that they were being watched and assessed.

Seeds of Affinity explicitly acknowledged the need to "ensure that everyone knows that it's a safe space for everyone and people have their vulnerabilities" (Chapter 4). In the context of women returning to the community following imprisonment, Fiona described the issue of women not feeling accepted, feeling judged, and therefore needing the proximity and emotional security of:

> a space for women to come together and feel a sense of community, feel a sense of togetherness and a sense of belonging ... it started by having women come together to have a shared lunch and just share experiences, a small group, which grew from there.

Having a physical space to come together, to share lunch, and to talk provided the emotionally safe space of acceptance and belonging, and the first step towards creating the conditions for women to start to feel empowered, to see themselves, and to be seen by others *as women*, not as criminalised women. The proximity required to break down the legal, moral, and social barriers faced by formerly imprisoned peoples needs to be grounded in physical space for these emotional, relational, and symbolic conditions to (quite literally) materialise. These conditions might be construed as a form of cultural safety[4] (Williams, 1999) – not least in terms of Indigenous culture – but also given the long shadow of stigma that can affect people's lives and shape their identity. Culturally safe spaces of listening and learning – without judgement, without "assault, challenge or denial" to/of a person's identity (Williams, 1999: 213) – implies creating space for ways of knowing and being in the world that are different from one's own. Working–making–doing together as co-producers can create this space, but requires letting go of authority and control, taking a risk. This may – indeed *should* – entail a degree of discomposure or feeling unsettled:

> [the] messy, unhinged, unanchored, adrift feeling that comes with collaboration, when you're not holding the reins.

Indeed, Johanna warns,

> if you're not uncomfortable you're not doing collaboration properly.

As a project involving imprisoned women, in a prison (which happened to be a men's prison) and that sought to allow women's voices and experience to be heard, Birds Eye View was perceived as risky in many ways. The political and institutional risk was the most obvious. In an election year, when law and order issues tend to become highly politicised, a government institution seen to be "allowing" women in prison to narrate their own stories, and for these to be available via a public podcast that would remain as a perpetual artefact, was politically perilous. The project's vulnerability to someone at the top [getting] cold feet" meant that Johanna bore the responsibility for the women's stories as an "unimaginably heavy" weight.

Risks were thus perceived and experienced in both directions: emotional risks for the women supporting other women, and political and organisational risks on the part of the prison and the government of the day. Some of these risks to correctional administrators were deflected by the co-production activities being grounded in the community, even where they traversed the prison boundaries. The slightly chaotic nature of the work and organisation of User Voice, for example, was offset by their demonstrated commitment to ordering chaos. Similarly, being outside the system (in some ways) gave Seeds of Affinity, like Birds Eye View, the space to grow as an organisation. The slow growth from a small group where everyone participated in discussions "at the table" carved out initial space for the project to develop. Conversely, the positioning of the Mothers' Project within a larger family research centre was viewed as a positive in that the project could be given the space to develop under the auspices of an established, well-regarded organisation. These examples illustrate the different ways space at the justice "table" was granted for different types of co-production activities.

What if

Co-production brings into play the "messy, unhinged, unanchored" realities of collaboration; the fact that those "in control" might have to relinquish that control, let go of their assumptions about their authority, share some of the decision-making power, and listen – *really listen* – to other people. This also means suspending perceived risks of failure – the fear of not doing it right, or making mistakes – and being open to uncertainty, *welcoming not knowing*, as an opportunity for learning how to do things differently. This is what co-producing knowledge in and between the spaces of criminal justice demands. Co-producers have the opportunity, through the work of co-production, to learn that *failing* is part of the learning process. Co-production demands the creation of safe spaces for learning in this way.

The case studies have shown what it takes to create physical spaces for co-production: places that are safe from a sense of being watched, observed, surveilled; places that are free of the usual criminal justice rules, constraints and controls, albeit in limited or temporary ways. Such safe spaces hold the possibility of liminal oases – temporary, in-between spaces that can allow people to be *other* than the labels of prisoner, offender or client, which they wear, for all other intents and purposes, in their criminalised context. Nielsen and Kolind (2016) suggest these institutional identities are "fuzzy", and that workers see people differently according to the context of their encounter. It is possible to imagine, therefore, that the creation of safe spaces where co-production takes place can also create the conditions where people see each other as *real people*. Making physical spaces safe for co-production is the first step towards creating spaces that are culturally safe for people to encounter each other, to engage in working–making–doing together, and to thus engender the proximity that is required for us to relate to each other respectfully as humans, and as equals.

Criminal justice intervention typically makes the strange and paradoxical demand of personal responsibility and transformation, on the one hand, and institutional obedience and structural compliance on the other. Creating interstitial spaces for people to grow and learn and develop is crucial for any rehabilitative or reintegrative goals to be realised. To achieve these inherently social and relational goals, these spaces must be equally and correspondingly social and relational. In this way, co-production in criminal justice, as a space-making site of collaborative pro-social activity, makes sense as a strategy for working towards one of the overriding aims of any criminal justice system: reducing crime by reducing reoffending.

The nature of these social spaces, however, goes beyond the physical space. Relationality requires trust, listening, and time and space for listening to unfold. This means making space made for story, for lived experience to be shared, listened to, and valued. This means reserving and giving space, as in The Mothers' Project, for "anybody – me included – who reaches the prison gates, arrives with their backpack of trauma and whatever that looks like" (Sinead). The questions then arise: Who owns that space? Whose territory does it become, whose Country, who is safe there? Who can tell their story? It is only in places of safety that people can begin to tell their own stories, to claim their identity.

Identity

In Chapter 2, we explored how, through criminal justice intervention, "offenders" become "active participants in their own punishment and correction" (Donohue & Moore, 2009: 320), locked into being both clients and offenders in a permanent state of liminality. This fragile state is reinforced by the inherently stigmatising and persistent criminal label, which forecloses other ways of being (Mbembe, 2015), other identities, and is hard to shift, even after prison (Johns, 2018). Like *time* and *space, identity* is a familiar concept when thinking and writing about people involved in the criminal justice system. Much has been written about the criminal identity, how this is formed and maintained, or renounced and redeemed (Maruna, 2001). Yet, people can have many identities (Stryker, 2008), albeit shaped by "available social roles" (Presser, 2008: 17) or an existing set of scripts (Goffman, 1963). These scripts shape the "kinds of people it is possible to be in a given society" (Stryker & Statham, 1985, cited in Presser 2008: 17). What is available to us will be in large part determined by the social context, by who has the power to both define those roles.

Prison is a very specific social context that permits a highly restricted set of roles. For the imprisoned – separated from family, familiar environments, and the capacity for expression of their other roles, such as parent or worker – this can result in a sense of separate and conflicting inside versus outside identities (Tripp, 2009). For many, this identity is further buttressed by community responses: criminalised people are framed in simplistic and one-dimensional ways, as perpetrators, offenders or, at best, *ex*-offenders, with justice involvement having lasting impacts on their citizenship, including voting rights, access to employment, and other supports. As an example, criminal record checks, present in many jurisdictions, are a specific barrier to employment, and being able to access a more legitimate role/identity (Aresti *et al.* 2010). It is in this context that co-production is situated. We turn now to how notions of identity were revealed in the case studies. Often these were evident in the explicit aim/s of the projects, as well as in less obvious ways. Four sub-themes were identified which capture these more subtle elements: blurring roles; co-production as recovery; acceptable identities; and disrupting narratives. Again, we follow this discussion with a brief consideration of the *what-ifs*, of how co-production may be harnessed to challenge and disrupt justice-defined identity.

Blurring roles

As outlined in Chapter 1, the blurring of distinctions or roles – removing the distinction between professional staff and service users – is argued to be core to co-production. Across all case studies such blurring was evident, but was also compounded by workers bringing additional personal and/or professional justice-related experiences to their roles. In Keeping on Country, Sarah and Beau were co-researchers as well as members of the community being researched. In Youth Justice, Tim was the researcher, but also a Department of Justice employee. Sinead, Fiona, Garry, and Mark all incorporated their personal experience of having been in prison into their formal researcher/worker roles with their respective projects. And while Claire was motivated to become involved in Straight Talking by her personal experience of a previous partner's recurring imprisonment, alongside her criminal justice-related social work practice, Johanna describes being disillusioned with a career in research and seeking to find a different way to elevate hidden and authentic stories.

Perhaps because of this, in our case studies, clearly delineated professional/non-professional roles and identities were uncommon; everyone had a backstory that complicated this dichotomy. Each backstory grounded individual motivations, as evident in the time and energy people invested in each project. For Claire, Straight Talking was the "culmination of a professional and personal journey … drawing on a range of experiences, relationships, ideas, and interest groups". This journey included taking the risk in recent years of revealing her personal experience with the justice system: "before that I don't think anyone would have been ready". Sinead similarly drew from her personal experience and her studies in social work to arrive at a PhD and the Mothers' Project. Doing this work – co-production – is not routine in criminal justice; it happens because the person/people with the backstory make it possible. As we've shown, they invest time and commitment, and get things done, but carry largely unseen costs. It is these very backstories and motivation that are harnessed and put to work in Justice co-production. Indirectly, the case studies suggest some acceptance that this is simply the cost of doing this work. Claire from Straight Talking, did, however, name this issue, highlighting that projects need to ensure that they actively support peer worker careers, and not just exploit them "to do the dirty work, as ... the volunteers at the grassroots".

The hidden costs – to those with a backstory, both financial and emotional – of doing co-production work were clearly outlined across all case studies. We noted the financial burden described by Sinead in our earlier observations about time: that co-production projects are often bounded by, and funded according to, official time but take up much more unofficial relational time. Fiona described Seeds of Affinity's formerly imprisoned co-founder Linda as having her phone on "24 hours a day. She's answering calls through the night ... all on a volunteer basis". The "exhausting" (Sinead) and "unimaginably heavy" (Johanna) weight carried by those working in co-production is brought about by doing what co-production principles suggest: blurring distinctions, sharing power, and, as Johanna says, getting "uncomfortable" to ensure they are "doing collaboration properly". These things are typically done alone, however, with limited supervision or support, hearing and working with stories of significant trauma, whilst managing their own backstory and championing co-production.

Co-production as "recovery"

In sectors such as mental health and drug and alcohol treatment, co-production activities are positioned (at least partially) within an individual recovery framework (Slay & Stephens, 2013). In criminal justice practice and scholarship, however, this paradigm is only hinted at in terms such as rehabilitation, reintegration, restoration, re-entry, resettlement, desistance, and – in Indigenous community terms – healing. With perhaps the exception of forensic mental health, *recovery* as an ongoing, non-linear process is generally not central to criminal justice practices. Yet in our case studies, recovery – including recovery of a "pro-social identity" – is a recurring theme. This is mirrored in the desistance literature, where generative opportunities to "give back" and help others (Maruna, 2001; Maruna & LeBel, 2003) are seen to have individual rehabilitative benefits.

Birds Eye View (Chapter 4) aimed to support participants to develop confidence and capacity for individual change. Seeds of Affinity – in giving back to the community via their social enterprise, community education and making prison packs – re-positions women; it allows them to take on a help-giving (active, empowered) rather than help-receiving (passive, disempowered) role (Maruna & Le Bel, 2003). In other case studies, this strengths-based or assets-based orientation of building on people's existing capabilities – one of the foundational tenets of co-production (e.g. see Slay & Stephens, 2013) – was evident, though in less obvious ways. For example, in Straight Talking, men in prison or on parole/community orders, while not directly involved in mentoring, provided direction that helped shape the development and implementation of the project. In a different way, in Youth Justice, young men's voices were specifically sought to understand *identity* from an inside perspective. In both instances, these co-producers could be considered help-givers, either directly or indirectly.

It is also evident in some case studies that the rehabilitative nature of co-production lay not only in the opportunity to inhabit and be seen and legitimised in a helper role but also in its capacity to offer space to participants to reconstruct the story they narrate about themselves. A powerful example of that is in User Voice, where men – whose *imposed story* (Hall & Rossmanith, 2016) tends to be of violent or recidivist offenders – relabel their criminal justice involvement as the destructive consequences of significant childhood trauma, emphasising the false dichotomy between victims/offenders (Smith & Kinzel, 2021). Mark Johnson speaks eloquently of the "emotional deprivation at the heart of the problem" of crime and justice. In seeking to redress this emotional deprivation, by humanising and building empathy for the other, recrafting personal narratives through the prism of recovery or rehabilitation carries emancipatory potential, yet also personal costs. Recasting one's identity involves trading on a personal story in ways that can mean relinquishing some parts of it. Personal stories can become public property, harnessed to the narrative vehicle of redemption. Even when driven with a degree of agency, challenging the prevailing one-dimensional view of "offenders", some risk of the commodification of individual and collective pain remains. Othering may persist.

Acceptable identities

As discussed earlier, under *time*, some of the case studies (Straight Talking, for example) suggest that access to co-production requires the justice-involved to have turned over a new leaf, to have reformed, to be "ready" and able to share their life lessons, their *lived* experience (past tense). "By making themselves appear 'redeemed', their criminal record paradoxically is a mark of authenticity" (Smith & Kinzel, 2021: 100). In contrast, *living* experience (present tense) may be perceived as still too risky, acceptable only as long as the person is contained, confined, still behind bars (as in User Voice, Birds Eye View, or Youth Justice). This requirement to identify and to be seen as redeemed – as authentically *"ex"* – is shaped by the justice context and the audience it seeks to address. Who is permitted to participate is often limited to those whose narratives comply with that of the *redeemed subject* and who, as indicated in the Birds Eye View case study, provide stories of positive role models but also of the negative consequences of actions. People's stories – their personal pain, childhood trauma, the pains of imprisonment, and how they have redeemed themselves – are put to work as a message to others. The way identities are constructed or curated to fit an ideal version of lived experience is, on the surface at least, emblematic of how pain and adversity can be commodified in the business of rehabilitation, which trades on success stories. For those already marginalised and traumatised by their life experiences, this can be re-traumatising. Yet the case studies also show examples of care and respect for people's voices and experiences, such as how the women in Birds Eye View maintained editorial control of their stories and how they were told, suggesting co-production affords opportunities for the expression of human authenticity.

Harnessing the redemptive narrative, with its warning for others, is partly what sets Justice[5] apart from other co-production settings. As noted above, in mental health, for example, recovery is central, and setbacks are an accepted and normal part of the process. As suggested earlier, in our discussion of *time* and *being ready*, in Justice, there is no relapse permitted, not when offending is simply seen as a bad choice (Weaver, 2011) and when your place at the table is reliant on your identity as an *ex*-offender. While Justice, to some degree, understands and embraces the notion of identity as a process of becoming (Presser, 2008) (evident in efforts across many youth justice jurisdictions to divert young people from the system, from being labelled as criminal and then living up, or down, to that label), the becoming remains linear: from *offender* to *ex-offender*. In the case studies, this was particularly evident in Straight Talking (discussed earlier regarding readiness and risk), where mentors needed to meet strict criteria, including no longer being on parole; they needed to be identified as firmly in the "ex" category. What is deemed an *acceptable identity* for a co-producer is shaped in part by the type of offence people have committed. This also played out in Straight Talking, as discussed earlier in *space,* in terms of how sex offenders were deemed too risky to be engaged as peer mentors.

The boundaries around what is *an acceptable story to tell* are shaped by Justice. Tim noted, in Youth Justice, that detention centre staff often acted as gatekeepers, sending him only the "easy" kids, to shape what story could be told, and hence presented publicly. In contrast, he also notes that they would sometimes suggest young people who they perceived to be more challenging. Tim understood this not as offering a deeper counter-narrative but to make his work, and the accurate gathering of the diversity of young people's experiences, more difficult. This informal gatekeeping by Justice can not only shape the narrative content – by narrowing the sample – but can also diminish the strength, scope, and perceived veracity of the evidence produced. Push back against these boundaries, where possible, was evident in some case studies. For example, as noted, User Voice advocates for input from all-comers, with the express aim of prisoners learning about democratic participation. In a similar way, the Birds Eye View project navigated through administrative and legal requirements to ensure that women's stories were told in ways that were authentic (but not defamatory).

Disrupting narratives

Despite these challenges, co-production, at its heart, relies on seeking out and working with a plurality of evidence, different ways of knowing. When co-producing knowledge *about* criminal justice, *with* people involved with the criminal justice system, this relies on engaging with and valuing the lived experience that comes from criminal behaviour/identity, even if this is only the label that has been applied by the justice system. Too often, of course, this label is amplified by a lasting social stigma, manifest in the suspicion and denigration of people currently (or formerly) imprisoned; as noted in the User Voice case study, in some prison officers' views, "prisoners did not deserve to have a voice" (Schmidt, 2013: 16). The case studies suggest the process of co-production in these criminal justice settings seeks, at times, either directly or indirectly to challenge identity, both how participants are perceived by others and how people perceive themselves. It can act to interrupt the dichotomies (good/bad, offender/ex-offender), discussed earlier, by valuing and incorporating the expertise of those with lived/living experience.

In Birds Eye View, there was an explicit aim to challenge narratives, both those of the women themselves and of the wider community. Through the co-production *process,* the project sought to engage women in different roles, expose them to new skills and experiences, and through this process to see different *possible selves* (Markus & Nurius, 1986). Having a podcast as the specific *product* allowed women to review, reframe, and present their personal narrative to a public audience, in an empowering and enduring way, as an artefact that lasts through time. This product sought to challenge existing community stereotypes of women in prison (it shows women as human: funny, relatable, understandable, with all the same concerns for their relationships, family and so on).

While we cannot comment on any direct or measurable impact on the community, this podcast fits into a wider and growing discourse about women in prison as criminalised (rather than inherently "criminal"), and commonly victims of abuse in both child and adult relationships. There is, however, at least one example of a changing individual narrative in the public domain: Rocket, one of the participants, now includes the label "storyteller" in her Twitter handle. Similarly, women involved in the Mothers' Project named this study in a way that prioritised their identity as mothers, rather than prisoners. In doing so, they not only challenged the centrality and legitimacy of the offender label but also staked a claim on their possible selves – selves they can see and expect to (re)inhabit, forging a connection with others, fulfilling a pro-social role. This connection supports their continued work with an informal network of activists and professionals in the community, well beyond the formal conclusion of the project in 2018.

User Voice, encouraging participation in prison councils from as many people as possible, not necessarily the best-behaved prisoners, forces prisons to confront differing narratives, to have a wide range of perspectives at the table, and to have to collaborate to develop workable solutions. As noted in that case study, research on prison councils has shown their success. On a practical level, User Voice councils have achieved positive outcomes, with the approval and implementation of the majority of recommendations made. But perhaps more importantly, success can be measured in how the council process has allowed prisons to see prisoner representatives (and prisoners, by extrapolation) as real people, and council members, rather than as "offenders". In turn, this shapes how people can see themselves as civic contributors. The implicit absorption of these changed narratives is likely at the heart of the councils' successful collaborations and outcomes. In these three case studies, we see not only a process of "reworking a delinquent history into a source of wisdom" (Maruna, 2001: 117), or an "edge", but also an acknowledgement by the criminal justice system/representatives of the importance of that wisdom, as well as the potential for that re-crafted story to frame and scaffold personal recovery.

What if

Our case studies illustrate that co-production under the Justice umbrella intersects differently with notions of identity, and in limiting ways, compared to other settings. The Justice conceptualisation of offending as a choice, and rehabilitation as a linear process with no room for mistakes or backsliding, can restrict who is considered an acceptable co-producer, and when they are deemed "ready". Furthermore, we see covert use of the backstories or identities of the professionals involved in these co-produced projects, and the hidden costs they carry in doing this work. However, our examples also reveal how co-production can be harnessed to challenge the power of Justice to define individuals and constrain knowledge production.

It is to these *what-ifs*, the explicit potential for co-production, to which we now turn.

Engaging in the *process* of co-production provides participants with an opportunity to act in a different role, to step out of their fixed institutional identity. Having access to this different script can allow people to build a sense of capability and a range of skills to bolster and build alternative narratives, or preferred stories about who they are, in ways that are complex and holistic. And importantly to have this "other" role acknowledged and validated. Akin to our earlier discussion of *time*, and the capacity of co-production to loosen the grip of Justice and to operate in a more human and relational temporality, *what if* one of the intentional aims of co-production was to enable Justice (and subsequently people themselves) to loosen its grip on a fixed and limiting "offender" identity and label? What if *recovery* was embedded as a core principle of Justice? What if there was an acceptance of people as multi-faceted, and participation itself was seen to build capacity for civic engagement and rebuilding of alternative stories and identities, rather than being a prize offered at the end when you have demonstrated that you are an "ex", that you are ready?

And what if the goal of co-production was to challenge not only the existing narratives held by individuals, communities, and Justice itself, about those in contact with the system, but also the evidence that is needed to drive change in the criminal justice system. As User Voice's Mark Johnson says: "We are the evidence". What if co-production, "standing between the pillars of reform and revolution" (Weaver, 2011: 1041), has the capacity to tilt the balance of power, in ways that can bring about genuine shifts in our understandings and practices of Justice? The evidence is growing that co-production has the capacity to be more than what Rose and Kalathil (2019) call a *collision of knowledges*; research into User Voice prison councils shows the benefits of wisdom gleaned through lived experience. Such benefits arise not through collision, but through mutual encounters.

Notes

1　For Iparraguirre (2015: 614), "cultural rhythmics" include the daily rhythm of life; the relationship between seasonal, celestial, and climatic cycles; music, myth, and narrative; economic, political, and work rhythms; and the tensions between urban and virtual rhythms.
2　This article (and others by the same authors) decentres human "authority" by naming Country as lead author.
3　Curiously, the term "on the wing" describes the sections of the prison where prisoners are housed in cells, yet also evokes the image of being in flight, as a bird, juxtaposing different embodied, spatial aspects of captivity and freedom.

4 Williams (1999: 213) defines cultural safety as "an environment which is safe for people; where there is no assault, challenge or denial of their identity, of who they are and what they need. It is about shared respect, shared meaning, shared knowledge and experience, of learning together with dignity, and truly listening".

5 Our discussion has led us to the sense that Justice in terms of the multiple inter-connected network of actors, agencies, and agenda that comprise the "criminal justice system", and the logics that conflict yet connect and sustain its flows, has a presence that overshadows everything, every action, and interaction that takes place within its purview. For this reason, from here on, we refer to "Justice" (capitalised) as both ethos (the character of) and entity (a character in) in this book's narrative arc. We develop this idea in the next and final chapter.

References

Anderson, D (2016) The value of 'bearing witness' to desistance, *Probation Journal*, 63(4): 408–424.

Aresti, A, Eatough, C & Brooks-Gordon, B (2010) Doing time after time: An interpretative phenomenological analysis of reformed ex-prisoners' experiences of self-change, identity and career opportunities, *Psychology, Crime & Law*, 16(3): 169–190.

Balint, J, Evans, J, McMillan, M & McMillan, N (2020) *Keeping hold of justice: Encounters between law and colonialism.* Ann Arbor, MI: University of Michigan Press.

Bawaka, C, Wright, S, Suchet-Pearson, S, Lloyd, K, Burarrwanga, L, Ganambarr, R, Ganambarr-Stubbs, M, Ganambarr, B & Maymuru, D (2015) Working with and learning from country: Decentring human author-ity, *Cultural Geographies*, 22(2): 269–283.

Brown, AM (2017) *Emergent strategy: Shaping change, changing worlds.* Chico, CA: AK Press.

Brown, M (2009) *The culture of punishment: Prison, society, and spectacle.* New York: NYU Press.

Collins, S & Long, A (2003) Working with the psychological effects of trauma: Consequences for mental health-care workers, *Journal of Psychiatric & Mental Health Nursing*, 10: 417–424.

Davis, A (2003) *Are prisons obsolete.* New York: Seven Stories Press.

Dawes, G (2016) *Keeping on country: Doomadgee and Mornington Island recidivism research report.* Townsville: North and West Remote Health.

Dawes, G & Davidson, A (2019) A framework for developing justice reinvestment plans for crime prevention and offender rehabilitation in Australia's remote indigenous communities, *Journal of Offender Rehabilitation*, 58(6): 520–543.

Dawes, G, Davidson, A, Walden, E, & Isaacs, S (2017) Keeping on country: Understanding and responding to crime and recidivism in remote Indigenous communities, *Australian Psychologist*, 52(4): 306–315.

De Sousa Santos, B (2014) *Epistemologies of the south: Justice against epistemicide.* Oxon/New York: Routledge.

Donohue, E & Moore, D (2009) When is an offender not an offender?: Power, the client and shifting penal subjectivities, *Punishment & Society*, 11(3): 319–336.

Dufourmantelle, A (2018) *Power of gentleness: Meditations on the risk of living.* New York: Fordham University Press.

Foucault, M (1977). *Discipline and punish: The birth of the prison.* New York: Pantheon Books.

Goffman, E (1963) *Stigma: Notes on the management of spoiled identity.* Hoboken, NJ: Prentice-Hall.

Guenther, L (2013) *Solitary confinement: Social death and its afterlives.* Minneapolis, MN: University of Minnesota Press.

Habdankaitė, D (2017) Delay as (non)foundation of bureaucracy, *Filosofia*, LXII: 59–73.

Hall, M & Rossmanith, K (2016) Imposed stories: Prisoner self-narratives in the criminal justice system in New South Wales, Australia, *International Journal for Crime, Justice & Social Democracy*, 5(1): 38–51.

Iparraguirre, G (2015) Time, temporality and cultural rhythmics: An anthropological case study, *Time & Society*, 24(3): 613–633.

Johns, D (2018) *Being and becoming an ex-prisoner.* Oxon/New York: Routledge.

Liebling, A & Maruna, S (2005) Introduction: The effects of imprisonment revisited. In A Liebling & S Maruna (Eds.), *The effects of imprisonment*. London/New York: Routledge, pp. 1–29.

Markus, H, & Nurius, P (1986) Possible selves, *American Psychologist*, 41(9): 954–969.

Maruna, S (2001) *Making good: How ex-convicts reform and rebuild their lives.* Washington, DC: American Psychological Association.

Maruna, S & LeBel, T (2003) Welcome home? Examining the "reentry court" concept from a strengths-based perspective, *Western Criminology Review*, 4(2): 91–107.

Mbembe, A (2015) *Decolonizing knowledge and the question of the archive.* Johannesburg: Wits Institute for Social and Economic Research, University of the Witwatersrand.

McNeill, F (2019) *Pervasive punishment: Making sense of mass supervision.* Bingley: Emerald Publishing.

Medlicott, D (1999) Surviving in the time machine: Suicidal prisoners and the pains of prison time, *Time & Society*, 8(2–3): 211–230.

Nielsen, B & Kolind, T (2016) Offender and/or client? Fuzzy institutional identities in prison-based drug treatment in Denmark, *Punishment & Society*, 18(2): 131–150.

Ó Tuathail, G (1996) *Critical geopolitics: The politics of writing global space.* London: Routledge.

Presser, L (2008) *Been a heavy life: Stories of violent men.* Chicago, IL: University of Illinois Press.

Rifkin, M (2017) *Beyond settler time: Temporal sovereignty and Indigenous self-determination.* Durham, NC: Duke University Press.

Rose D & Kalathil J (2019) Power, privilege and knowledge: The untenable promise of co-production in mental "health", *Frontiers in Sociology* 4(57): 1–11.

Schmidt, B (2013) User voice and the prison council model: A summary of key findings from an ethnographic exploration of participatory governance in three English prisons, *Prison Service Journal*, 209: 12–17.

Slay, J & Stephens, L (2013) *Co-production in mental health: A literature review.* London: New Economics Foundation.

Smith, JM & Kinzel, A (2021) Carceral citizenship as strength: Formerly incarcerated activists, civic engagement and criminal justice transformation, *Critical Criminology*, 29: 93–110.

Stryker, S (2008) From mead to a structural symbolic interactionism and beyond, *Annual Review of Sociology*, 34: 15–31.

Stryker S & Statham A (1985) Symbolic Interaction and Role Theory. In G. Lindzey & E. Aronson (Eds.), *Handbook of social psychology*, Vol. 1, 3rd ed. New York: Random House, pp. 311–378.

Sykes, G (1958) *The society of captives: A study of a maximum security prison.* Princeton, NJ: Princeton University Press.

Tripp, B (2009) Fathers in jail: Managing dual identities, *Applied Psychology in Criminal Justice*, 5(1): 26–56.

Tubex, H (2015) Reach and relevance of prison research, *International Journal for Crime & Social Democracy*, 4(1): 4–17.

Weaver, B (2011) Co-producing community justice: The transformative potential of personalisation for penal sanctions, *British Journal of Social Work*, 41(6): 1038–1057.

Williams, R (1999) Cultural safety – What does it mean for our work practice? *Australian and New Zealand Journal of Public Health*, 23(2): 213–214.

8 Now what?

[The] messy, unhinged, unanchored, adrift feeling that comes with collaboration, when you're not holding the reins.[1]

This book started with questions: What is co-production in criminal justice contexts? What or who makes the "co" in co-production? And what makes co-production in and about criminal justice unique or distinct from co-production in other contexts? These are questions we have grappled with, explored through the case studies, and to which we return here, at the end of this book. In the previous chapter, we analysed the case studies through the conceptual lenses of *power and hierarchy* and *ways of knowing*, and identified themes of time, space, and identity in examining co-production in practice. In this chapter, we continue our analysis, moving beyond the case studies, to think more broadly about the pitfalls and challenges of co-production in criminal justice. We reflect, finally, on the principles and possibilities we have gleaned through working–making–doing this book together, and what they might mean for producing knowledge about criminal justice *with* people entangled in criminal justice.

Our approach is both practical and conceptual. We have looked at what people *do* (practices) and what people *think* (the underlying meanings, ideas and assumptions) when co-producing knowledge in/about criminal justice. We approached the case studies with a methodological lens that privileged the telling of each project's story while acknowledging that not all stories have been told. Delving deeply into different examples has allowed us to move beyond *what should happen* in co-production, to conceptualise *what does happen*, to identify the pitfalls and possibilities for others. The case studies suggest that the reality of co-production means iterative, often messy processes of negotiating temporal, spatial, and relational boundaries and differences, and meeting people *where they are*, and that these occur at the speed of trust, according to cultural and relational rhythms. The case studies show that co-production is not one thing. There are many ways of doing it.

DOI: 10.4324/9780429328657-11

What or who makes the "co" in co-production?

Chapter 1 opened with a definition of "co" as a prefix denoting working–making–doing *together*, *jointly*, *mutually*, and *indicating partnership or equality*. The question of who or what makes the production of criminal justice knowledge "joint" or "mutual" points to our discussion below about the omnipresence of Justice,[2] not least in terms of who holds power to decide. But we can also see, through the case studies, that there are different ways people and projects *do* push and stretch the constraints of Justice, working collaboratively, to bring together different ways of knowing what we know. We consider these briefly now as a kind of continuum, a diversity of practices, illustrating varying degrees of reciprocity or mutuality, partnership or equality.

Collaborative workers

Reflecting on *what or who makes the "co" in co-production*, people's orientation towards knowledge and their relations with the people they are working with are key. For some, knowledge is always partial and gaining a full perspective and deep understanding means taking in different points of view. Some projects were not initially framed as co-production at all, yet might accurately have been conceptualised in co-production terms. In the Youth Justice case study, for instance, Tim valued reciprocity and the opportunity for young people to tell their stories, to convey their perspective on things that matter to them. His genuinely respectful listening skills and professional experience enabled him to work relationally. He assumed young people's expertise in their own lives, which is a clear and powerful statement given the statutory relationship between imprisoned young men and a worker in "the system". It signals a degree of power-sharing. It recognises the limits of adult knowledge about young people's perspectives on the world, how adults always look back, down, and through a different temporality. It suggests that co-producing knowledge means learning to see from below and outside the ken of those *doing the looking*.

This case study reveals the overlap between practices that are labelled co-production and participatory approaches that produce knowledge in collaboration with research participants. We are suggesting here that something that is *not* conceived or identified as co-production can still generate co-produced knowledge. Sinead, for instance, initially rejected the co-production label because the Mothers' Project did not fully incorporate the stages of co-design, co-planning, co-delivery, and co-evaluation. This raises the question: When is co-production *not* co-production? Ascertaining the boundaries of "co-pro" is not straightforward; perhaps it becomes easier when its instigators engage explicitly, intentionally with power and partnership, such as those we have come to think of as champions and innovators.

Champions and innovators

The combination of personal insight and professional training oriented towards social justice and reflexivity can be a powerful motivator for collaborative approaches to knowledge-making, as Straight Talking suggests. This case study also clearly shows how power relations remain firmly and rigidly ordained by the Justice hierarchy: the clear separation between those with official "decision-making clout" and professional influence and those without – the "have-nots" – while allowing the latter "to have a voice" (Arnstein, 1969: 217). As a professional with Justice influence, Claire's role in bringing forth the "co" in co-production was to bridge these rungs on the hierarchy. Yet, despite the creativity embedded in Claire's idea of Straight Talking, the freedom to involve peers in supporting peers and to work collaboratively (as she imagined) was constrained by this rigid power structure and its bureaucracy.

The case studies involving imprisoned women were similarly circumscribed by Justice yet showed less restriction on collaboration. In terms of what and who made the "co" in Birds Eye View and the Mothers' Project, Johanna and Sinead embarked on collaborative relationships with women early on in their projects. Birds Eye View began with co-conception, gradually involving women in the co-development and ultimately co-creation of the podcast as a lasting artefact of the women's experience. This included substantive roles including co-editing and, importantly (given it extended beyond the project timeline), co-promotion of the podcast in the public arena. Birds Eye View thus gave women opportunities to participate in a project about their experience, to be recognised as partners, to decide how their stories would be presented, and to be heard as experts in their collective story. Designing projects grounded in people's lived experience, and working together as partners, was thus one way that people did the "co" of co-production. This was motivated by a firm belief in the rights of criminalised people – as citizens – to have a voice and participate in things that affect them. For these projects' champions and innovators, the opportunity for "better justice" or "improved services" always appeared secondary to this deeper rationale.

Keeping on Country exemplified a broader political agenda in terms of non-Indigenous co-producers explicitly championing the principle of self-determination for First Nations peoples. While the research brief very much reflected government priorities and language, on the ground the project was described as a partnership from the outset. The non-Indigenous expert researchers and clinicians, Glenn and Andrea, saw themselves as co-researchers with local community members, Sarah and Beau. From the beginning the project was defined as co-production, bringing multiple knowledges – different ways of knowing – together. This was done on community terms: Sarah and Beau selected activities and insisted on taking everything back to their communities in a careful, iterative process of communication, going back and forth, checking, from the preparation of questions to the reporting of findings. It would be problematic, in the context of Australia as a settler-colonial state, to elide the obvious power dynamics arising from two white researchers working with Indigenous communities. But, acknowledging that we live and work on unceded land and that historically unequal power relations shape ongoing relations, the non-Indigenous researchers demonstrated a strong personal and professional commitment to social justice, power-sharing, and action.

Rebels and entrepreneurs

There are different kinds of activists in Justice: one is the lived experience activist, an opportunity-seeker and risk-taker who resists or opposes the established order. User Voice's Mark Johnson is a prominent example. Based on his own life experiences, including being helped and supported in his recovery by peers, together with his entrepreneurial skills and drive, Mark has led the development of a national organisation, employing many others with similar life experiences to his own, and bringing about changes in how prisons and probation services operate. Seeds of Affinity co-founder, Linda was similarly self-directed (with the support of co-founder and parole officer, Anna). These examples represent a certain "type" that we describe as the *rebel entrepreneur*, who carries their lived experience as a torch, illuminating injustices they have experienced and lighting the way for others. This type[3] is perhaps most likely to drive co-production from the ground up, by pressing for lived experience to be recognised and valorised as expertise, to change both attitudes and practices.

Of the case studies we examined, User Voice embodies a full co-production story, beginning with the intention to create an organisation run for, by, and with ex-offenders. Its operation in high-security prisons ironically subverts the pervasive risk logic of criminal justice; sometimes, as we describe below, the "tightness" of the prison may contribute to a corresponding "looseness" in the constraints on the project. Perhaps it permitted the chaotic nature of the organisation to be contained and thereby perceived as less risky in broader Justice terms. Birds Eye View – another prison-based project – embodied this looseness in a different way.

Although it was similarly characterised as slightly chaotic, it was a project that unfolded organically, gathering high levels of peer involvement as it went. The entrepreneurial aspect of this collaboration is evident in how a storytelling project initially aimed at reducing alcohol-related harm evolved into a podcast, elevating authentic stories previously unheard. The way this project was conceptualised and implemented encouraged "rebels" to find their voice in legitimate ways they may not otherwise have found.

Summing up the what and the who

The "co" in co-production can be driven by individual motivations, pragmatic concerns about exclusion and inequality, and broader aims of transforming social relations. The "co" implies working–making–doing *with* people with lived/living experience of crime or criminalisation. But as our earlier discussion and case studies show, the categories of *expert by experience*, *lived experience worker*, and other professionals are blurry and not necessarily mutually exclusive. They overlap in various ways. Thinking about the "wounded healer" motif that often accompanies lived experience, for example, User Voice clearly illustrates this category with so many of its workforce having been criminalised and imprisoned themselves; but so too does Claire in Straight Talking (having previously been the partner of an imprisoned man). In Seeds of Affinity, Fiona had been in prison and is now a volunteer and social work graduate. In this way, the case studies exemplify perspectives from inside, outside, and across the us-and-them divide. Identifying these different roles – collaborative workers, champions and innovators, rebels and entrepreneurs – leaves the question for all of us seeking to co-produce: who is most able to disrupt the status quo, challenge power and hierarchy, and bring forth different ways of knowing?

This question reminds us, from our discussion in Chapter 2, that whoever is *doing the looking* is holding the power to define (both problems and solutions). Working together in mutual partnership, to bring forth different ways of knowing as equal in value, therefore requires looking from below and within; looking through and past established boundaries. Learning to see from below does not require any special permission or power. It does require a commitment to imagining things differently and to challenging how things are. It means recognising power where it exists and acknowledging that inequalities may stymie genuine participation. The challenge is how to name and meaningfully engage with power when it is both palpable and diffuse, both obvious and invisible. The power structures and dynamics and the us-and-them categories that characterise Justice create unique conditions for co-production. "Contestation over punishment is constant" (Smith & Kinzel, 2021: 102), yet we tend to smooth over and silence these moral questions by looking/acting through a technocratic, evidence-based, managerialist lens. The role of co-producers is to credential storytelling, to valorise lived experiences and counternarratives of social harm and State coercion, and, ultimately, to humanise Justice.

The omnipresence of Justice

The question of what makes co-production unique in criminal justice reminds us that existing co-production principles and practice guidelines draw largely on lessons from mental health, which tend to focus on relations and interactions at the individual level. Our analysis broadens this focus to take in the wider context of norms, assumptions, and attitudes towards justice-involved people. In Chapter 7, we applied the lenses of *power and hierarchy* and different *ways of knowing* to the case studies, exploring themes of time, space, and identity. Running through these themes is an underpinning and overarching presence: Justice itself, the system, its workings and imperatives. We think of Justice as a widespread, ever-present, intangible entity; an atmosphere, milieu, set of conditions; a territory, without a single fixed place, yet that permeates and suffuses many spaces. In all our conversations, our case studies, this amorphous presence of Justice was always *felt*. That is not to say it was uniformly experienced. While Justice was always there, hovering over, in, or behind every project, its manifestations varied. When we consider what makes co-production distinct in criminal justice contexts, we conclude it is this inescapable mesh of legal, moral, administrative, and discursive threads: *the omnipresence of Justice*. We explain this omnipresence and how Justice pervades or shadows co-production in our case studies under three headings: *risk, bureaucracy* (and its settler-colonial logic), and *lived experience* as an identity.

Risk

Risk permeates every facet of Justice. Every interaction is mediated through the lens of risk, from decisions about who is granted access to certain places, to the use of risk assessment instruments designed to measure an individual's likelihood of reoffending according to population-based statistical modelling. This actuarial logic seeps into and shapes the assumptions embedded in everyday decision-making, creating a self-perpetuating risk logic loop. This is how the omnipresence of Justice manifests in diffuse yet fundamental ways. The case studies showed how projects were variously shaped and constrained by the omnipresence of risk and risk-management thinking, including about how to do co-production and with whom. This was most obvious in Straight Talking, where certain groups of people were excluded from being mentors in the project (convicted sex offenders, those on parole) due to considerations of risk both real and perceived. But it was also apparent in how – by not accepting government funding – Seeds of Affinity sought to separate itself from Justice, its constraints and KPIs.

Projects that had been funded by the governmental arm of Justice, or had received ethics or access approval to do their work within one of its institutions, found themselves in a situation where they were being given enough rope to undertake the exploratory, unconventional work needed to establish relationships for co-production. Indeed, we found it telling that these case examples – all except Seeds of Affinity – were the same examples where those who led them had already been vetted as "safe", not risky, already implicitly trusted to know that they should not take that step too far, or in the wrong direction. At the same time, they were very aware that if they were to overstep these limits – or indeed go in the "wrong" direction – the retraction on that rope would be swift and consequential. As Johanna in Birds Eye View put it, there was always a sense of that project being vulnerable to the whims of "someone at the top" getting "cold feet".

Decisions about who is deemed risky, based on their history, lifestyle, or criminal record, show how Justice looms large, shadowing people's lives in concrete and material ways. Yet we see that the most serious risks and safety needs are those borne by the criminalised people at the heart of each case study. For the men and women efficiently dispatched via "Con Air" to prisons more than 1,000 kilometres away from family and community, for example, being released to the liminal space of return, often without support or resources, leaves them vulnerable to reimprisonment. For women released without the support of a welcoming community, such as Seeds of Affinity, the reality of poverty and social isolation due to a persistent criminalised identity can lead to loneliness and despair. User Voice employees know, from their own experience, what this feels like, and that these risks are often beyond an individual's control. For people with this lived or living experience, the risk of making a mistake, the assumption or expectation of failing (again), is never far away. Justice is thus a *risky* omnipresence in many people's lives. The risk for criminalised people as co-producers of criminal justice knowledge – if the source of their knowledge is not treated with due care or *gentleness* (Dufourmantelle, 2018), if Justice cannot bear witness to itself – is that they might be set up to fail.

The way risk both holds and folds around people's lives recalls Foucault's (1976/2012) "mesh of power" and how it monitors, controls, and *disciplines*. Earlier we raised the question: When is co-production *not* co-production? As our case studies hinted, there is a palpable and ever-present risk that Justice powerholders can label activities co-production as a box-ticking exercise, without shifting any decision-making power to the hands of co-producers; without ever letting go of the reins. Thus, in ostensibly *managing risk* by maintaining control, Justice *produces risk* for co-production projects by delimiting the possibilities for reciprocity, mutuality, genuine, or equal partnership. The intertwining threads of risk, power, and hierarchy – specifically the power of Justice bureaucracy – thus constitute the mesh of power that Justice casts. This mesh is experienced individually, in existential and everyday ways, recalling notions of "grip" and "tightness" (Crewe, 2011; Crewe & Ievins, 2021). This mesh is also felt collectively: in the risk of co-option, the risk that *co-pro* becomes just another Justice programme.

As co-production terminology becomes increasingly normalised, the ever-present risk of discursive co-option is in some respects an inevitable, largely benign example of neoliberal expansionism, part of the surface layer omnipresence of Justice in our lives. At a deeper level, however, it signals the manifold dangers of reformism. As transformative agendas are subsumed under the guise of political pragmatism, emancipatory values and aspirations can be rendered seemingly trivial, impractical, and irrelevant to the unassailable rationale and continuity of the Justice juggernaut. As co-production becomes part of a Justice reformist agenda, it risks becoming a tick-box exercise, or worse, what we might call *faux co-pro*. For instance, as Scotland's Children and Young People's Commissioner recently observed:

> Some very strange examples of "co-production" being discussed at the moment. If you have very limited involvement of young people and then ignore their views, you can't call it co-production just because they were in the room.
>
> (@Bruce_Adamson, Twitter, Jun 3, 2021)

When co-production smacks of tokenism, or the empty ritual of *non-participation* (Arnstein, 1969), the risks are high. People whose life experiences are commodified in this way risk being invisibilised: their voices silenced, their knowledge subordinated, their existence further marginalised.

Bureaucracy (and its settler-colonial logic)

As we wrote in Chapter 2, one of the main threads constituting Foucault's mesh of power is *rationality*, embedded in the assumption that reality is *programmable*, and that individuals and populations can be regulated through their *knowability*. Justice maintains its grip through these rationalities and the practices arising out of them. How is this grip felt? In a correctional context, it can be experienced as "tightness": "oppressive yet also somehow

light ... like an invisible harness" (Crewe, 2011: 522). For many, Crewe
and Ievins (2021) contend, this invisible harness can feel heavy, onerous,
invasive; for others, in certain situations, being "held or contained" (p.64)
might feel assistive, even reassuring; where it is felt too loosely, through
laxity or inconsistency, some can feel "abandoned and invisible" (p.62).
Graeber (2016) suggests that bureaucratic rules hold all of us in a sense of
safety, predictability, the comfort of knowability. Crewe and Ievins (2021:
65) suggest that the tightness of this "institutional grip" is tolerable *only*
"when it is supportive rather than coercive, and where it recognises and
maintains the integrity of the individual". Arguably, however, Justice is
always coercive. We are alert to situations where institutional attention
may be welcome, but precisely and only because of its absence at other
critical moments in people's lives, as women's traumatic histories attest
(in Chapter 4), for instance. In these circumstances, the omnipresence of
Justice risks standing in for genuine human relationships and relational
bonds, its grip always limiting possibilities for self-determination.

The omnipresence of Justice bureaucracy is a feature of settler colonisation, as Keeping on Country shows. The project's funding, timelines,
and parameters, not least its focus on recidivism, signify the bureaucratic
reach of Justice as an arm of the State, and its power to *look at* and define
the problem *of* or *for* (rather than *with*) First Nations people. The governmental grip of Justice is most obvious in its harms – penal sanctions that
mean people are imprisoned and released miles from their Country, for
instance – yet equally diffuse and far-reaching in its more benign manifestations, including government-funded research projects. That is not to
impugn the genuine, respectful, and collaborative work of the Keeping on
Country researchers, whose approach demonstrated a sincere commitment
to embracing and valuing different ways of knowing and relating to each
other. It is to acknowledge the wider political-cultural context.

That is, there are forms of knowledge – and ways of producing it –
that fit neatly into spreadsheets, timelines, budgets, evaluation protocols,
and government reports. These bureaucratic frameworks tend to dominate the gathering and accumulation of criminal justice knowledge: the
statistics, data, and "facts" that inform the policies and practices that
govern, control, or otherwise impinge upon the sovereignty of colonised
peoples.[4] In all these ways, the omnipresence of Justice is felt, resisted,
and negotiated by Indigenous peoples constantly, from everyday interactions with authorities to political decision-making. First Nations voices
are still too often mediated, measured, and judged according to settler
standards of what is and what should be. In this context, the challenge
for co-producers is to push against the grip of assumptions, the tightness
of institutional strictures and bureaucratic structures, and work into the

spaces in between. In this way, co-production can loosen the hold and the homogenising tendency of Justice by opening spaces for multiple ways of knowing to be valued equally.

We have observed (in Chapter 7) the temporality of the Justice bureaucracy and how control is exerted through the power of *delay* (Habdankaitė, 2017). The frustrations of the "risk-bureaucracy" and its inconsistency are especially noticeable in prisons (Crewe & Ievins, 2021: 53), where delay functions as a reminder that bureaucratic power shadows human lives. Delay is not just about the management of time and space, though. Delay also creates shadows, waiting places, and pockets of time, and it is in these fuzzy spaces of in-betweenness that co-production can take place and – more importantly – claim space. For example, our case studies hinted at the ways that participating in the co-production process often lessened the burden of imprisonment for those involved, at least temporarily. The women in the Mothers' Project and in Birds Eye View, in Chapter 4, spoke of the levity, lightness, and laughter these projects generated for them. We might say, then, that co-production holds possibilities for loosening the grip, lessening the weight of the omnipresence of Justice, at least for a moment. But our case studies also hint at ways that co-production can potentially transfigure people's lived experiences of Justice, ways that are not so fleeting.

Lived experience as an identity

The stigma of criminalisation and punishment can disfigure a person's identity for life (Goffman, 1963). Our case examples suggest, however, that co-production processes can loosen the grip of Justice, the tightness of its hold over criminalised people's lives. What stood out in all the examples we considered was how involvement in these projects allowed for new stories to be told, and for new purposes to be found. We saw this in Seeds of Affinity, for example, where women were empowered to "gain an identity other than being criminalised women" (Fiona). The Birds Eye View podcast similarly provided some of the women an escape route to an alternative identity such as "storyteller". But particularly striking was the User Voice example, where being a formerly imprisoned person now involved in the co-production of knowledge about imprisonment – in prison, with other prisoners, through prison councils – offered a portal to a new identity: a *lived experience* identity. As Garry from User Voice put it, the life experiences that had led to criminalisation and punishment now gave him an "edge" to his work and life as a self-proclaimed ex-offender. His insider knowledge became his credentials. User Voice illustrates that for some people the tightness of Justice's invisible harness can shift "from something to be endured" into "a personal project or occupation" (Crewe, 2011: 522). Thus, in co-production projects, encounters with Justice – typically oppressive, constrictive, constraining – can also hold liberatory potential.

This is not to laud encounters with Justice, however, or to minimise the deep scars they can leave. The case studies highlight the fragility of the *lived experience* identity as one often grounded in trauma, shame, and humiliation, and forever shadowed by risk. Lived experience both holds and conceals this fragility. It is vulnerable to the risk of relapse, failure, or burn-out, as alluded to in Birds Eye View. Yet its vulnerability is masked by its emergence as a category, its embodiment in individual lives, and, through the accretion of these layers, its solidification as *an ongoing thing*. It becomes a social identity with currency; it carries credentials. Staking claims to this identity – such as User Voice's claim: "We are the evidence base" – shores up its validity, but also hides its vulnerability. The commodification of lived experience risks further effacing its fragility as a social identity. We see this in Straight Talking, where people suspended in an in-between zone of acceptability, their inclusion in the program being conditional upon their being "good" (whatever that means). Lived experience as an identity is thus performed and performative; it may yield approval, even applause, yet always risks a swift return to condemnation and exclusion.

Perhaps the tenuousness of the lived experience identity gives rise to a willingness to play the game, as it were, as a pathway to perceived and certified success. Perhaps the past experience of being stigmatised as unworthy because of a criminalised identity, which then becomes the thing translated into something seen as worthy, makes tolerable the possible tension between being a co-producer, being responsibilised for oneself, and the subsequent governing of others (recall Foucault's idea of governing – we return to this below). Perhaps this is what Crewe and Ievins (2021: 65) mean by institutional tightness being experienced as "supportive rather than coercive":

> where it recognises and maintains the integrity of the individual through authentic engagement with his or her full personhood rather than trapping him or her in the amber of the past.

Being seen *as a whole person*. Perhaps, under such conditions, the contrast of the coercive grip of penal control makes the loosening of the harness feel like freedom. And perhaps, compared to having been ignored and silenced, the opportunity to participate in knowledge production about the experience of coercion – and being listened to – *feels like* authentic engagement. In this way, the lived experience identity provides a pathway into an imagined future.

Stigma is one of the most distinguishing features of co-production in Justice compared to other settings, such as mental health. While the stigma of mental illness and the power of the State to impose involuntary detention under mental health legislation evoke similar power dynamics, the difference lies in the construction of people's identity in terms of their past and future behaviour *and* their moral character. The medical conceptualisation of mental illness – seeing the "patient" as ill and in need of care – allows for treatment and recovery. An "offender" may similarly be pathologised for their behaviour. Yet the aims of punishment and denunciation work against the supposed rehabilitative aims of Justice and therefore counter the possibility of recovery. Instead, Justice demands that a person rehabilitates and redeems themselves – and *demonstrates* their rehabilitation and redemption – as an *ongoing* project, all the while bearing the stigma of criminalisation, which persists long after punishment supposedly ends. The key feature of co-production in criminal justice settings, then, is the focus on the Justice subject – the *offender client* – as a perennially risk-bearing individual, distinct from a patient or otherwise designated recipient of "care". Certainly, mental illness can still carry a stigma. Yet a medical record does not diminish a person's decency, integrity, morality, or trustworthiness as does a criminal record. And such status, once lost, is hard to regain.

The omnipresence of Justice metastasises through language. Justice constructs identities that are indelibly marked by the stigma of criminalisation: people become offenders or prisoners; then ex-offenders and ex-prisoners. The stickiness of criminal labels makes them difficult to remove. The omnipresence of Justice similarly pervades the language of co-production. Think of how alternative identities – "service user", "consumer", "lived experience [person]" – are made available and normalised in Justice discourse. When these terms are used uncritically, unthinkingly, and become normal through everyday usage, they become a way of rebranding the stigma of criminalisation. They smooth over how and why people are criminalised. They disguise institutional harms and colonial violence (inflicted through punishment, control, neglect or abandonment), and they impose a common-sense logic of rationality and choice, rendering these harms *individual* problems. Individual problems require individual solutions, which implies a degree of freedom to choose that may in fact be tightly constrained. In this respect, talking about "equal partnership" can obscure persistent underlying inequalities and give the impression that deep-seated structural disadvantages are surmountable by individuals having enough grit and determination, and simply choosing the right pathway. Language governs by constructing and normalising identities that can become totalising. Thus, being labelled a professional, credentialled "ex-offender" risks becoming a pathway out of one form of criminal othering into another.

What are the possibilities for co-production in criminal justice?

Our intention in writing this book was to identify current understandings of the key elements and principles of co-production in criminal justice. What has been revealed is confusion, contradiction, and complexity. There is confusion over terms and definitions: what is and isn't co-production. There is contradiction between aspirations towards freedom and encircling forms of control, and between pledges to partnership and persistent, unyielding hierarchies. And there is complexity in multiplicity, in the fact that co-production is *not one thing*; that working–making–doing together inevitably and always involves competing demands, collisions, and compromises between different ways of knowing and being in the world. In raising these points, we bring cautious optimism to practitioners and project leaders aspiring to co-produce knowledge in and about Justice. We use language intentionally to challenge assumptions about everyday notions, such as criminal justice, and to think differently about *what we know* and about questions of identity, belonging, and otherness. We see possibilities for co-production in disrupting dominant constructs of criminalised people – either as "unworthy" or as "consumers" providing a commodifiable type of "evidence" – and, instead, creating space for people to narrate their own stories. By bringing multiple perspectives and experiences into play, co-production expands knowledge, inviting new insights and deeper understandings, and challenging limited ways of seeing.

We've gathered examples – albeit a small selection – to show what co-production can be. We offer these stories (and our interpretation of them) as possibilities to explore through further practice and experimentation. Co-production is about *doing*. It's about trial and error. Co-production is risky and requires imagination and a commitment to working–making–doing and *learning* together, allowing uncertainty to unfold. It takes time. It requires patience, trust, and gentleness. It demands relational engagement based on proximity, meeting each other as humans, not as parts of a system or machine. This is a challenge when working within the constraints of Justice and its risk bureaucracy. It's also a challenge in terms of criminal othering. As formerly imprisoned Paula (2021) warns, co-production "cannot start with 'the other' and preparing 'the other' for the process"; it must be a mutual encounter. But what of the institutional grip of Justice, and the risk of co-production being co-opted into a reformist agenda, of becoming only ever an improvement strategy? What can *co-pro* do to disrupt power relations that are so deeply entrenched? The case studies show what might be possible.

Expanding accountability

Justice-making hinges on accountability: holding someone to account for their wrongful behaviour. Being accountable to each other is also key to working in a mutual trusting relationship, which – as we have seen – is required for genuine co-production to unfold. In the first instance, this means acknowledging the hidden costs of co-production, borne by individuals who invest the time, care, and emotion in the relationships on which co-production depends. It demands that Justice takes account of this investment and provides adequate support for this role. Certainly, this form of relational accountability can germinate and grow in the in-between spaces of Justice. But genuinely mutual encounters between co-producers demand relations of equality that Justice cannot bear or allow. This kind of relational engagement – for it to even manifest, let alone becoming generative and normative – requires holding Justice to account, demanding that *Justice bear witness to itself.*

More broadly, this means demanding that governments, policymakers, decision-makers, funders – all those invested with the State's power to punish – acknowledge that the hold of Justice over people's lives often *works against its implicit aims* to right wrongs, to address the harms of crime and violence. To achieve these aims means halting the ever-expanding scale and reach of Justice, shrinking its footprint; it means acknowledging the capacity for communities to participate in the everyday work of justice-making, and making room for this to happen. The possibilities for expanding notions of accountability from the individual to the relational arise out of the central principles of participation, partnership, and power-sharing. These are not merely reformist add-ons. These principles are pathways to thinking differently, together, human-to-human, in mutual encounters.

Out of mutual encounter arises the possibility of relational accountability: seeing each other as interrelated, *in relationship*, understanding the obligations and fulfilling our roles in that relationship (Wilson, 2001). In this way, co-production holds the possibility – as our case studies and others attest – of shifting the ground of relations between people. Only by doing this at the local level can larger transformations unfold. Certainly, decoupling the juggernaut of Justice from the machinery of the settler-colonial state is no easy task. But each time a co-production project works into the in-between spaces of Justice and stakes its claim to those spaces, there is the possibility of expanding these out, making them larger, making Justice able to hold multiplicity and difference, gently.

Space for lived experience

Making, holding, and keeping space for truly collaborative knowledge-making to unfold begins in physical space. In the case studies, holding the keys (literally and metaphorically) signified the recognition of co-producers as trusted partners. Co-production projects created opportunities for doors to open both inwards and outwards – even prison doors – as the User Voice, Straight Talking, and Birds Eye View examples showed. In User Voice and Straight Talking, lived experience provided credibility among others deemed offenders, while emerging leadership, the capacity to listen, and a willingness to share their expertise provided their professional credentials. It was through working–making–doing things together that their lived experience could be articulated in their collective voice. This voice becomes louder and clearer as these practices proliferate. As our case studies show, co-production thus makes it possible for co-producers to claim space for lived experience to be valued and valorised as a crucial insider perspective. Recalling Foucault's *lutte de pouvoir* (power struggle), the verb *lutter* (to wrestle) evokes the sense of how this often inevitably means an ongoing wrestle for power, wrangling space to do this work together.

Symbolic space is, of course, as important as physical space for lived experience to be treated with care. The world of Justice divides people into two categories: those who offend and those who are offended against. This binary does not hold, yet still it persists. Co-production invites collaboration that, in many ways, undermines this categorisation. Producing knowledge together requires *seeing* each other, recognising and relating to one another as equals. Being accountable to each other. Criminal justice services are grounded in control and the power to punish (Weaver, 2011). Co-production gives space for this power to be loosened, for workers to push at the edges, stretch the boundaries, to relinquish *power over* people. Co-production can claim space that allows people to *see each other as people*, exposing the false offender/non-offender dichotomy and revealing that we all are *equally human*.

Room to make mistakes

Clearly, there are plenty of risks involved with co-producing knowledge in/about Justice, on all sides. For criminalised people, the risk of failure adheres to a criminal record like an unshakeable shadow. For powerholders, sharing power with those over whom they have previously exercised power risks ceding some of their own. Professionals may fear that valorising lived experience will diminish their expertise. Co-production champions and innovators risk their efforts being co-opted by Justice and subsumed into its reformist agenda, thereby further entrenching settler-colonial carceral logic. This logic undergirds carceral responses that paradoxically *cause harm* while seeking to address the harms of crime and violence. The risk for co-production as an emancipatory, democratising practice is that it becomes a buzzword, hollowing out these larger transformative aspirations. In each scenario, trust is the first and last casualty.

If we take heed of the rebel entrepreneur, though, these risks become a challenge to be taken on rather than avoided. We have shown that co-production is not one thing. And that co-production is in the doing. Learning to co-produce means learning by doing. Guiding principles are an important starting point, as a kind of safety harness. But at some point, it is necessary to just get on with it and see what is possible. The real safety harness is the space to learn and make mistakes. This requires trust. Time is needed to build trust, to recognise the humanity of the other; mutual encounter by mutual encounter. Echoing Tim's words, this needs to be slow and long-winded and people need to be able to make mistakes and not be judged.

Taking time

Time, and the time it takes to do things, is one of the ways the omnipresence of Justice is felt. We see this in Keeping on Country, in how bureaucratic city time was normalised through project timelines and fly-in fly-out schedules. Yet by *Keeping on Country*, literally, this project was able to rescale this tempo, to alter its speed and the proximity to its Justice context, requiring the co-producers to move lightly, gently, slowly. As an example of slow storytelling, Birds Eye View similarly shows how working–making–doing together can and does take time; the time needed to work at the speed of relationships, the speed of trust. Through mutual encounter, sharing stories, and working–making–doing together, thereby building trusting relationships, self-sustaining support networks such as those generated by Seeds of Affinity and User Voice can emerge that will outlast any single co-production project.

Co-production brings forth the possibility to adjust the tempo of justice-making to match its place and context, to honour its purpose and engage respectfully with its partners and participants. This is what it means to meet, to encounter each other in relation, as citizens. In prisons – where important aspects of citizenship have been withdrawn – opportunities to enact and practise citizenship allow people time to see and make a future beyond prison. In communities, opportunities for people to see each other, to listen, to learn by working–making–doing together, over time, can break down otherness, can build trust. The stigma of criminalisation and imprisonment can last a lifetime. Re-tempoing Justice according to co-production rhythms can allow for pathways to acceptance – as returning citizens, and holders of knowledge – to unfold. This unfolding is possible as long as mutuality, partnership, and equality are – at the very least (to use Paula's words) – the destination. Creating these possibilities is incremental, it takes time, relational time, transformational time.

Notes

1 As Johanna described in Birds Eye View, Chapter 4
2 The criminal justice system comprises an interconnected web of relations; multiple systems of interrelated practices, meanings, processes. We use "Justice" as shorthand for this complexity.
3 Though ex-prisoner activism and organisation is far more well-established in the United States, we note several examples of organisations led by formerly imprisoned people in the Australian Justice landscape, including abolitionists Sisters Inside, penal reformers Justice Action, and First Nations support organisation Deadly Connections.
4 We note the push for "data sovereignty" led by Indigenous scholars in Australia and beyond; see, for example, Maggie Walter, Tahu Kukutai, Stephanie Carroll Rainie, and Desi Rodriguez-Lonebear (Eds.) (2021) *Indigenous Data Sovereignty and Policy*. Oxon/New York: Routledge.

References

Arnstein, S (1969) A ladder of citizen participation, *Journal of the American Institute of Planners*, 35(4): 216–224.

Crewe, B (2011) Depth, weight, tightness: Revisiting the pains of imprisonment, *Punishment & Society*, 13(5): 509–529.

Crewe, B & Ievins, A (2021) 'Tightness', recognition and penal power, *Punishment & Society*, 23(1): 47–68.

Dufourmantelle, A (2018) *Power of gentleness: Meditations on the risk of living*. New York: Fordham University Press.

Foucault, M (1976 [2012]) The mesh of power (trans. C Chitty), *Viewpoint Magazine*, September 12, 2012.

Graeber, D (2016) *The Utopia of rules: On technology, stupidity, and the secret joys of bureaucracy*. Brooklyn/London: Melville House.

Goffman, E (1963) *Stigma: Notes on the management of spoiled identity*. Hoboken, NJ: Prentice-Hall.

Habdankaitė, D (2017) Delay as (non)foundation of bureaucracy, *Filosofia*, LXII: 59–73.

Paula (2021) Thoughts from Paula. In *Prison: A place for co-production*, UCL Public Engagement Blog, January 18. https://blogs.ucl.ac.uk/public-engagement /2021/01/18/prison-a-place-for-co-production/

Smith, JM & Kinzel, A (2021) Carceral citizenship as strength: Formerly incarcerated activists, civic engagement and criminal justice transformation, *Critical Criminology*, 29: 93–110.

Weaver, B (2011) Co-producing community justice: The transformative potential of personalisation for penal sanctions, *British Journal of Social Work*, 41(6): 1038–1057.

Wilson, S (2001) What is Indigenous research methodology? *Canadian Journal of Native Education*, 25(2): 175–179.

Appendix
Our approach to analysing the case studies

The analytic process took place in stages. We commenced our preliminary analysis with the three women's case studies (see Chapter 4), inductively generating 12 categories that we framed as questions, each with a series of sub-questions. We subsequently used this framework deductively, to code the remaining case studies. The 12 categories and the questions arising from them are as follows:

- Problem definition: what is/are the problem/s and who's defining it/them?
- Time and temporality: is there a temporal component?
- Partnership: what is the nature of the partnership?
- Roles: what roles are being performed/undertaken?
- Space/place: what are the spatial elements?
- Language: how is co-production articulated, verbalised, spoken of?
- Co-production activities: how does it manifest?
- Voice: how is "voice" conceptualised?
- Story: who has ownership of "story"?
- Risk: how is "risk" perceived and managed?
- Trust: how does trust manifest?
- Motivation and back story: what are these for different people/roles/participants?
- Other emerging themes?

Table 1.1 shows the full thematic coding frame, including all sub-questions. Oriented theoretically by notions of power and hierarchy, and ways of knowing, we distilled these elements into three major themes in the data: *time*, *space*, and *identity*.

Table 1.1 Co-production case study thematic coding frame

No.	Code	Theme	Prompts
1)	**Problem definition**	**What is/are the problem/s & who's defining it/ them?**	• The power to define (Who holds it? How does it manifest? Who lacks it?) • A hierarchy of knowledge (Are different forms of knowledge apparent? Are they valued differently? Is some knowledge privileged? Subjugated? How does this manifest?) • How is power negotiated (in the context of problem definition)?
2)	**Time and temporality**	**Is there a temporal component?**	• What does the temporal aspect look like? Is there a history behind/ beyond this? e.g. is it a discrete project? What are the time frames? What's ongoing? • Is the "problem" conceived as emerging or perpetual? Why is it a problem *now*?
3)	**Partnership**	**What is the nature of the partnership?**	• What is the time frame – does it have a beginning, middle, and end? • Is it an ongoing relationship? • Who's included (i.e. who are the co-producers)? • What is the relationship to "justice" (actors, institutions, organisations, processes)?
4)	**Roles**	**What roles are being performed/ undertaken?**	• What is the role of "justice" (individuals, institutions, organisations, systems, government, funders, etc.)? How is "justice" present? • How is the role/presence of "justice" mediated through other roles or individuals?
5)	**Space/place**	**What are the spatial elements?**	• Where are activities taking place? e.g. creating "safe space"; in community; on Country. • What is the significance of space and place? • What does it intersect with – gender, history, etc?
6)	**Language**	**How is co-production spoken of, verbalised, articulated?**	• What verbs do people use? What is the language of co-production? • What "co" words come up – e.g. co-conception, co-creation, co-development, co-edit, co-present, etc.?

(Continued)

Table 1.1 (Continued)

No.	Code	Theme	Prompts
7)	**Co-production activities**	**How does it manifest?**	• What are the mechanics of co-production? e.g. consultation • What do people *do?*
8)	**Voice**	**How is "voice" conceptual-ised?**	• How is "voice collected/gathered"? What's done with it? • Whose voice? Who gets to *speak?* Who gets to *be heard?* • Who has the right to be heard? • The authority to speak – who is granted it, by whom, under what conditions? • What is the relationship between voice and story?
9)	**Story**	**Ownership of story**	• Whose story? Who owns it? • What stories *are* told? What stories *can* be told? • What is *meant* to be told – is there an ideal story? • What stories *cannot* be told? What parts of a story get "cleaned up", laundered, sanitised in making the "product"? • How are stories made palatable/ laundered?
10)	**Risk**	**How is "risk" perceived and managed?**	• How and where does risk manifest (for *all* participants)? • What are the risks to/for workers? Institutions/organisations? • What are the risks to/for people with lived experience? • How is risk managed by individuals in different roles? By institutions/ organisations? • What are the risks of/ with telling stories – who tells them? How are they told? • What do people risk in telling and/or "trading on" their stories (when their lived experience is their currency)?
11)	**Trust**	**How does trust manifest?**	• How and where does trust manifest (for all participants)? • What does trust mean for individuals in different roles? For institutions/ organisations? (What are relations of trust and what do they rely on? What makes relationships *trusting/ trusted?*)

(Continued)

Table 1.1 (Continued)

No. Code	Theme	Prompts
		• How is *risk* mitigated through trust?
		• What role do relations of trust play (between individuals, for institutions) – e.g. is there a "charismatic" or trusted leader?
12) **Motivation and back story**	**What are these for different people, roles, or participants?**	• How do people's motivations feed into the co-production process?
		• What's the personal investment? (And how does it shape people's role in the process?)
		• How important is *care* and *caring* (*for* and *with*) as a motivation?
		• How is care made possible through this project (i.e. what does it permit, enable, create the opportunity for)?
		• What other motivations are discernible?
13) **Other**	**Emergent themes?**	• What else comes out of the case study?

Index

For Product Safety Concerns and Information please contact our EU
representative GPSR@taylorandfrancis.com
Taylor & Francis Verlag GmbH, Kaufingerstraße 24, 80331 München, Germany

www.ingramcontent.com/pod-product-compliance
Lightning Source LLC
Chambersburg PA
CBHW061744270326
41928CB00011B/2369

9 7 8 1 0 3 2 3 0 6 0 6 3